TWO RIVERS

The Power of Collaboration and Other Leadership Lessons

SHERY ROUSSARIE AND
KELLY MACKEN-MARBLE

ISBN: 978-1-960146-18-2 (Hard Cover)
         978-1-960146-19-9 (Soft Cover)

Edited by: Melissa Long

Published by Warren Publishing
Charlotte, NC
www.warrenpublishing.net
Printed in the United States

To Collin: you are important beyond words.
Your wisdom has always exceeded your years.
As with no other person, you see me.
You've given purpose to my path.
— Shery

To my husband Daren: thank you for
believing in me even on the days
I didn't believe in myself.
— Kelly

Where two rivers meet, the waters are never calm.
—A Ugandan proverb

It is the outstanding collaborators [who] enjoy the long careers because bringing out the best in others is how they found the best in themselves.
—Margaret Heffernan,
"Forget the Pecking Order at Work" TED Talk, June 16, 2015

INTRODUCTION

This book is the natural continuation of a collaboration between two people leading two fiercely competitive companies, each moving on a parallel trajectory toward individual organizational success. These leaders looked beyond the singular to create something greater than either could have done alone. This story involves navigating challenging (occasionally forbidding) waters where rivers converge, at times exhilarating, at times terrifying. The two leaders interrupted and disrupted strategic designs of other competitive organizations to the extent that threats and manipulative behaviors became the expected. Proponents toasted the leaders and opponents cursed them, signaling that the long hours, difficult discussions, and sensitive navigations encountered along this journey were the lighted path leading to the positive impact envisioned at their first meeting in 2018.

Shery

I am Shery, one of the collaborators sharing this story. Today I am gloriously retired and enjoying my life's work from the periphery through service on boards of health care related organizations, as well as supporting leadership development and sustainable physician independence. My education and the last thirty years of my work are in health care, which I entered through a linear albeit rambling route. My dual degree is a master of health care administration and master of business administration, and although I didn't start out on this path, it is the one that chose me and has been an exceptional roller coaster of a career. Shortly after graduate school, I providentially stumbled onto the managed care track of health care. Managed care is that part of the health care industry that brings physicians, hospitals, and insurers together to help reduce costs to employers. Starting in Texas, I made my way to Arizona before landing in Indiana. In my eighteen years in managed care, I worked with amazing physicians whose concern for quality and successful patient outcomes was their innate driver. In 2007, I had the honor of becoming the chief executive officer of one such physician group.

During the course of my career, I have been blessed to have relationships with leaders in the community, in health care, and in other industries. The warm welcome I received when I first arrived to the Midwest touched me and deepened my desire to do likewise for others. So when Kelly moved to town to run the largest group of independent physicians, I reached out. We met for breakfast and immediately connected. Our goals for long-term viability were aligned: to keep independent physicians independent and to reduce costs to consumers. By the end of that first breakfast, we had a plan to create a new managed care network. Within six months, we were collaborating on three major initiatives, each of which could stand alone but together they were market changers. By mid-2020, our companies had created a managed care company, purchased a small physician-owned hospital, and merged our physician groups. It was epic. And it caused epic shifts in the local health-care market's tectonic plates.

Kelly

I am Kelly, the other collaborator or partner in crime in this story. The path that led me to my current position, like for many of us, was a winding one. Coming from a family of health care providers, I went to nursing school first. After spending two years caring for my youngest child, traveling to large health systems across the country, and being exposed to the real challenges patients experience, I changed my career focus to where I thought I could provide the most value—health-care administration. I completed a bachelor's degree in health-care management and a master's degree in organizational management. My early career was in Southwest Michigan supporting primary care and specialty physician practices in rural settings. In 2002, I took a leadership role for a health system in northern Minnesota and spent the next twenty years in various executive leadership roles supporting population health or value-based care initiatives as well as working with physicians to support inpatient and ambulatory care services. I began to think about the work I was doing and how I wanted to spend the last part of my working years. It's always been important to me to be in a role where I can provide value and make a difference regardless of title. In 2019, I made a significant career change, moving away from leading in large health systems to a role as CEO of a large, independent, multispecialty physician practice in Indiana.

I have been blessed to work in so many great organizations and with some amazing physicians and caregivers. Over the past four years, I've been honored to work with this incredible group of physicians who have provided care in their community for more than one hundred years.

Shery

The stage for our story was set long before Kelly and I met in 2018. It has been building over time as health care has become a bigger business and a major industry. Physicians, in working to keep up with the changing environment, found themselves falling into one of two categories: those who find safety in relying on corporate structure to lead their practice, and those who do not. The latter, the independent or self-employed physicians, own and run their own practices. All the decisions for the practice—when to hire additional physicians, what staff to employ, number of patients to see in a day, volume and types of surgeries to perform, and the like—are made by the physician. With rising costs of doing business and increasing regulatory requirements, more and more physicians are moving to a hospital-employment model. This migration has developed into fierce competitive strategies between hospital corporations and independent physicians. Where a physician is well established, the hospital sees an opportunity for growth by capturing all the business generated by that physician, things like hospital stays, surgical procedures, lab work, and x-ray services, and so aggressively recruits the physician. If the physician declines the hospital overtures and chooses to remain independent, the hospital hires a doctor from outside the area to directly compete with the independent physician. The result of this strategy is that choice (i.e., competition) is minimized when hospitals own the entire revenue stream, causing consumer costs to increase.[1] It is in this space that Kelly and I saw opportunity to build a stronger health care community by working collaboratively with each other, not just inviting but encouraging hospital systems to join us. Our collective knowledge and experience gave us vision to see a path where all players would still compete and where all could still grow. This strategy was built on creating products and service lines together while moving away from redundant practices like physician recruitment. This was a logical step to us, since our doctors already used the hospitals and were the loyal partners who facilitated the growth that the facilities had enjoyed. Yet each time we approached the hospitals, we were met with varying degrees of dismissal. So rather than give in to their demands of owning our individual companies or crumbling under their threats, we spent the next two years creating a reality of market-rocking possibilities. In short, we transformed the landscape.

We experienced that collaboration and cooperation between two strong, independent organizations with leaders whose vision aligned, resulting in one of the greatest disruptions this medical market has seen. Since collaboration and cooperation seem to be a rare strategy in any industry, we wanted to share how two competitors used those tools to build a robust and superior organization. The result is growth, strength, and vitality for innovators who recognize that working together produces

---

1 Christopher M. Whaley et al., *Nationwide Evaluation of Health Care Prices Paid by Private Health Plans: Findings from Round 3 of an Employer-Led Transparency Initiative* (Santa Monica: RAND Corporation, 2020), https://www.rand.org/pubs/research_reports/RR4394.html.

amazing outcomes. This book was written by two women who worked to save their companies and shook the ground under those who vowed to stop it. This is our story of how saying *yes* changes everything.

Mountaintops inspire leaders, but valleys mature them.
—Winston Churchill,
former prime minister of the United Kingdom

CHAPTER 1
Arm Wrestling or Rappelling

Shery

At any point in time, we are living into who we have become through our responses to life's curves. I got into health care through a series of unforeseen events, starting with a degree designed to lead me into a counseling career. I wanted to work with adolescent children. After about a year of working at a mental health hospital, I decided a business degree would provide me with broader career options that better met my evolving career goals. In the years before I finally pulled the trigger to start graduate school, I migrated into fundraising through nonprofit organizations. I was married to my college sweetheart, Mitch, a man with ruggedly handsome good looks and a kind spirit. After he finished nursing school, we moved to the Gulf Coast of Texas. We settled nicely into the beach lifestyle, relaxed and casual. He was a nurse, working in the critical care units of a large tertiary hospital and I was the market manager for a national nonprofit.

One July evening, Mitch and a couple of friends decided to go fishing early the next morning. He and one of his buddies stopped to catch bait off the access road of the interstate connecting Galveston to Houston, on their way to the other friend's house to prepare for the next morning's fishing excursion. About 10:30 that evening, I received a call that Mitch had been "hit by a car." Most details of that evening and the time that followed are lost in a fog, so I don't remember who called me—only that there were no answers about what had happened or what was meant by "Mitch has been hit," just that his friend was on the way to my house to take me to the hospital. Willing myself to not believe the worst, I reasoned that if he showed up in our Jeep, Mitch would be fine, and we would just need to get the car repaired; I would pick him up at the hospital, and we would be home late that night. I left our sleeping six month old with my high school aged brother-in-law while I headed to the emergency room.

Once there, I was not allowed to see Mitch as people who knew and worked with him were going in and out of the ER. The emergency staff was working diligently to stabilize him. Eventually, someone told me he had been directly hit by a pickup truck. The truck struck his right hip and threw him into the guardrail, which broke his ribs and punctured his lung but kept him from drowning in the brackish waters of the bayou.

The wetlands between Galveston Island and the mainland on I-45 are teeming with baitfish. Cars are often parked along the side of the access road with their occupants standing nearby, fishing pole or cast net in hand. Unfortunately, Mitch had chosen to cast his net from a bridge with no shoulder. Someone, who presumably spent an evening at the bar just south of where Mitch stood, was driving north on the access road with no lights. Mitch was hit, his friend was in shock from witnessing the accident, and the driver never looked back. An auto-pedestrian hit-and-run. In an instant, our lives changed. As far as I am aware, there was no attempt to identify the driver or the truck.

Mitch's injuries were extensive. He had a torn aorta—which typically has a mortality rate of between 80 and 85 percent—broken ribs, a punctured lung, a perforated bowel, and of course a crushed pelvis from the impact of the truck.[2] Mitch miraculously survived the hit-and-run, though it was a couple of months before anyone at the hospital was willing to say he might survive. The first few months

---

2 Wikipedia, "Traumatic Aortic Rupture," Wikipedia, Free Encyclopedia, updated October 22, 2021, https://en.wikipedia.org/wiki/Traumatic_aortic_rupture.

of his five-month ICU stay were the most crucial. I lost count of the number of surgeries he had during that time. The most critical issue that first night was to repair the torn aorta. He would survive nothing else if this could not be repaired. Thankfully, an amazing trauma surgeon was on call. She saved him that night; then she managed his care over the next five months and beyond.

While Mitch made it through that first night, his hospital stay was fraught with complication after complication. He became septic twice, had necrotizing fasciitis—commonly known as "flesh-eating disease"—spent months on a ventilator, and since his liver and kidneys were compromised, he was on dialysis twice during his stay. To allow his perforated bowel to heal, he was given a temporary ileostomy. This procedure created a hole, or stoma, through his side to redirect his small intestine contents for collection into a bag outside his body. The procedure was successfully reversed a year later, reconnecting his small intestine internally. During the hospital stay, the orthopedic trauma team made multiple attempts to repair the crushed pelvis, which they compared to a package of crackers that had been hit with a hammer. After a month or so of trying, the decision was made to remove his leg. This amputation is called a "hemipelvectomy"—Mitch lost his entire right leg and a portion of the right side of his pelvis.

The thing about Mitch's wounds that first night, and crushing orthopedic injuries in general, is that they are *bloody*. During his time as a trauma patient, Mitch had a total of eight hundred units of blood and blood products. According to the Red Cross, the average adult body holds ten units of whole blood.[3] Mitch's accident was in 1986, a year after the United States started testing the blood supply for HIV.[4] During the middle of Mitch's hospital stay, doctors thought it best to

---

3 "How Much Blood Is in the Human Body?" Whole Blood and What It Contains, American Red Cross, updated 2022, https://www.redcrossblood.org/donate-blood/dlp/whole-blood.html#:~:-text=adult%20will%20have%20approximately%201.2,10%25%20of%20an%20adult's%20weight.

4 Centers for Disease Control and Prevention, *US Public Health Service Guidelines for Testing and Counseling Blood and Plasma Donors for Human Immunodeficiency Virus Type 1 Antigen* (Washington, DC: US Government Printing Office, March 1, 1996), https://www.cdc.gov/mmwr/preview/mmwrhtml/00040546.htm#:~:text=Blood%20donations%20in%20the%20Unit-ed,%2D2)%20since%20June%201992.

test him since he had received so much blood. He had indeed received some tainted blood and was HIV positive.

Mitch finally returned home in December 1986, terribly thin, missing a leg, and HIV positive. He recovered well, resumed his love of fishing, and eventually returned to work. By this time, my career was beginning to take shape. I moved into health care marketing, first with the local hospitals, then for a brain-injury rehab center. Recognizing that Mitch, while outwardly healthy, was terminally ill, I determined after several years that it was time for graduate school to provide me with the best opportunities to eventually support myself and our child.

This experience with Mitch, while certainly different from anything I could ever imagine as we began our life's journey, enriched and enhanced my life in unanticipated ways. In the long hours of waiting to learn if he survived another night while at the same time caring for an infant turning into a toddler, emotional capacity and self-preservation filtered away minor irritations and petty complaints we all experience in our everyday work life, allowing only the most important matters to reach consciousness. Though admittedly I set it aside from time to time, walking through Mitch's accident, recovery, and death reordered my DNA, by and large. The resulting change, or perhaps the previously undiscovered depths that surfaced as a result of these events, manifested a new level of patience for the unknown stories of others along with an impatience for those who spend too much time focusing on the minutiae of life. Along this road I learned that everyone has a story; everyone has been through some trial. As managers, our role is to look over the heads of individuals, focus on production and outcomes, and ensure that the tasks get done. As leaders, we look into the hearts of the individuals to garner how we can best support others so they can best support the organization. Seeing people as integral to the roles and functions that make an organization operate with efficiency and viability versus seeing "my employees," a term of ownership too often used as a means to an end, simply a tool, expendable and replaceable, to accomplish the manager's goals. This difficult season of my life allowed me to view the world through the wider lens, step back and take in the vision of what could be, inviting collaboration and cooperation. With Mitch's multiple and significant injuries there were specialists from varying fields of study, each working on staying within that one single field to fix the problem they best knew how to repair. Once his survival and recovery was evident, the providers started working as a team and the coordinated care resulted in a path to returning home.

Despite the hardships during this time, I loved what I learned of health care and resolved that there is job security in this industry: health care will always be here regardless of what form it may take over the years. My goal in graduate school was to become a leader. I *knew* at a deep, instinctive level that leadership could be done better than what I had recently experienced. Silos within silos. Departments designed to work together led by people who clamored for the spotlight, either relegating their subordinates or outright stomping on them. How could an organization grow and rise above its competition if it could not communicate or work together within its own walls? In a future chapter, I will get into the story of the sticky-note manager and the flying vice president. Both of these people, while neither a model of leadership I desired, certainly influenced my leadership style. Poor examples of leaders drove me to pursue something more, to be something better.

While working as the marketing director for a brain-injury rehabilitation center, I entered graduate school. I took one class while working at the rehab, but when I realized it would likely take me more years than Mitch had left in his life to complete the dual master's, I left work and enrolled full time. I had completed the didactic portion of my degree and was a few months into my administrative residency when Mitch died. It had been six and a half years since his accident, and our child had just turned seven.

All our experiences change us, as stones tumbling beneath the roiling, rushing waters of converging rivers or underneath the slow but constant trickle of a stream. When you experience the death of someone this close to you, you are never the same. Some people might refer to such an experience as "gaining perspective." More than that, such loss provides the opportunity to look for what is important. When the flood waters of a river's rushing flow demolish all the walls around you, and you are left standing nakedly raw and bare, what's left behind is what means the most.

Another less dramatic, though still powerful, influence that informed my leadership style was Herb Kelleher, who built Southwest Airlines. I was coming of age in my career as he was growing Southwest. He shunned traditional ceremony and hierarchy. His unconventional leadership led to loyalty and success above the rest of the airline industry. He recognized it is the happy employee who generates a happy customer that results in a happy stockholder. His employees described him as "drawing you into a dialogue that made you feel smart, as though your ideas were good and worthy." One of his executive officers once said, "Herb, it's harder for me to get in to see you than it is for a mechanic, a pilot, a flight attendant, or a reservations agent." Half-jokingly, Herb said, "I can explain that to you very easily: they're more important than you are!"[5] But my favorite Herb Kelleher story is about his response to threatened legal action from a small company in South Carolina called Stevens Aviation, as described by the *Washington Post* in his 2019 obituary:

> At the time, Southwest's advertising slogan was "Just Plane Smart."
>
> The company said it was unaware Stevens Aviation already had the slogan "Plane Smart" as its motto.
>
> Mr. Kelleher proposed that he and Stevens Aviation Chairman Kurt Herwald settle matters with an arm-wrestling match.
>
> "Rather than pay a team of lawyers, Herwald and I decided to wrestle it out at the Sportatorium in Dallas," Mr. Kelleher said. "It was a hoot. The whole world focused on it. BBC called to interview me in London. I told them I was too busy training."

---

5 Kevin and Jackie Freiberg, "20 Reasons Why Herb Kelleher Was One of the Most Beloved Leaders of Our Time," *Forbes*, January 4, 2019, https://www.forbes.com/sites/kevinandjackiefreiberg/2019/01/04/20-reasons-why-herb-kelleher-was-one-of-the-most-beloved-leaders-of-our-time/?sh=3bc92271b311.

In photographs of his "training," Mr. Kelleher was shown lifting bottles of Wild Turkey in both hands as a cigarette dangled from his lips.

More than one thousand spectators attended the "Malice in Dallas" showdown.

"In the end," Mr. Kelleher said, "I got trounced."

But all was not lost. He and Herwald became fast friends, and they agreed both companies could share the "Plane Smart" slogan.[6]

Herb Kelleher's actions and resulting accomplishments further established my belief that competition does not have to be destructive and divisive. We can compete for the same physicians, patients, or programs and still shake hands or sit down together to figure out what will benefit the overall health of the patient and community.

Over the years, I have worked to build relationships with competitor CEOs. At one point, I challenged the CEO of a competing organization to rappel down the side of a building together for a local agency dedicated to the safety of area youth. I thought this fundraising event would be a great way to show the market that our focus is on the health of the community more than the health of our bottom line, and we might actually get some fun publicity out of it. My offer was declined. At another time when working at a hospital, I proposed we challenge the other hospital system to a baseball game. It would have been novel and fun! Moreover, events like these had the potential to bring us together in creative and competitive ways that just might result in collaboration. But these were not to be until Kelly moved to town. When I made the same rappelling challenge to Kelly, she readily accepted. She did so with such enthusiasm that I was later surprised to learn she has a significant fear of heights.

---

6 Matt Schudel, "Herb Kelleher, Visionary Co-founder and Chief Executive of Southwest Airlines, Dies at 87," *Washington Post*, January 5, 2019, https://www.washingtonpost.com/local/obituaries/herb-kelleher-visionary-co-founder-and-chief-executive-of-southwest-airlines-dies-at-87/2019/01/04/7d3160e2-1031-11e9-84fc-d58c33d6c8c7_story.html.

During my career, I also made more serious attempts at collaboration with our competitors.

An opportunity to run a physicians hospital organization (PHO) took me to the Midwest. PHOs are organizations that steer payers, employers, and patients to particular health care providers, and they are anchored around a specific hospital partner. I tried to engage the competition to open our networks. At that time, two particular hospital systems I was interested in were less than a mile apart and shared the same medical staff, which meant that the same physicians worked at both hospitals. Many cities in the Midwest had been spared the fate of larger cities where national health-insurance companies ruled over the health care market. This unique status was primed for the local PHOs to collaborate into a larger, citywide network while continuing to compete for hospital services. With this proposition in mind, I approached the competitor. The door for collaboration between the two PHOs would not open.

After I left the PHO and became the CEO of a physician group, I once again recommended a collaboration between the two PHOs. Again it was declined. I took the request all the way to the top leadership, who actually agreed. Unfortunately, within a week of that agreement, I received word that the hospital was withdrawing support of the PHOs working together. This self-protection significantly contributed to moving the PHOs toward irrelevancy. The competitor's steadfast decision seemed to come from a fear of losing business and relevance when, in reality, this strategy could have protected and grown each.

Over my thirty-year health care career, similar scenarios have repeated this pattern time and again in markets across the nation. It may be an approach for collaborating on a service—say, bariatric or cardiovascular services—or it could be on physician recruitment or program development. The hospitals tell us they are interested and willing, yet as discussions progress, the independent physician group is pushed aside and told the product, service, or providers must be owned by, named for, driven and controlled by the hospital. One example of this was around a laborist program.

The laborist concept is a relatively new one, gaining widespread popularity over the last ten years. This is where an obstetrician is on-site at the hospital twenty-four hours a day, seven days a week. This differs from the past, when a woman who did not have an obstetrician would show up at the emergency room, and an on-call physician would be notified. The woman and child would be monitored until it was time for delivery, then the physician would arrive at the hospital and deliver the baby. In this new system, when that same mother arrives at the hospital, there is an obstetrician on hand to assess the baby and mother. This, ideally, reduces complications for the mother and baby and eliminates the question of who will care for a pregnant woman who does not have a physician. Dr. Robert Olson, an obstetrician and gynecologist writing for Doximity, says of laborist programs, "[i]mmediate treatment or intervention leads to increased patient safety, which, in turn, can reduce bad outcomes, lessen malpractice situations, shorten hospital stays, and increase patient satisfaction."[7]

Obstetricians with Kelly's group and my group had been providing contracted laborist services for many years when it was time for contract renewal. The hospital led the negotiations. Both independent groups were assured that they had the same contract, and we knew we provided the same services. We requested that we negotiate together. The hospital equivocated and would only schedule meetings with groups one at a time. What should have been a simple renewal of a fairly straightforward contract dragged on for more than eighteen months. Contract extensions were added and renewed to keep the hospital and the physicians legally compliant.

The meetings we did have were circular. The hospital would tell us they were concerned for quality, yet they could not provide any instances of quality concerns or poor outcomes. They would cite

---

7 Robert Olson, MD, "The Birth of a New Option for Ob-Gyns: 'Laborists,'" Medical Business, Op-Med, posted June 8, 2018, https://opmed.doximity.com/articles/the-birth-of-a-new-option-for-ob-gyns-laborists-651ed98d-86d9-453f-8923-4c8652962850?_csrf_attempted=yes.

physician availability, yet we had the largest number of obstetricians to cover laborist calls and had no history of access concerns. The delay tactics were confusing and continued until the summer of 2018, when at the end of another long, circular meeting, the hospital stated that they had already hired two laborists of their own and they would no longer need the services of either independent group.

It became clear that the hospital failed to understand that these two groups had the largest number of physicians delivering babies at their hospital. These physicians have influence on a mom's decision of where to deliver her baby. The hospital had just cut off the groups who brought them the most patients who also happen to be the health-care decision makers for their homes. Establishing a loyal relationship with these mothers is essential for continued health-care brand loyalty throughout the life cycles of those families.

The firestorm that ensued after the hospital pronouncement involved both independent groups immediately terminating their agreements. Following a number of energetic conversations with hospital leadership, one of the contracts for a newly hired laborist was revoked, and our agreements were rapidly finalized. That is, until Kelly and I brought our two organizations together in collaboration. The two of us and all our physicians knew this agreement was short term and that the laborist contract would be revoked within a few years. As you will see in an upcoming chapter, collaboration between the two independent physician groups was not received well and accelerated termination of this agreement.

Collaboration does not mean giving up a competitive edge. Herb Kelleher exemplified the philosophy that successful results await creative approaches. When competitors challenge one another, both become better, just as iron sharpens iron.

We are leaders in the many and varied roles of our lives, whether it is in our companies, our volunteer roles, or within our families. The position you hold is less a determinant of leadership than your approach to others. When you have the opportunity to lead a committee, a team, or a project, envelop your mind in how you can do it differently, creatively. Consider:

- Meeting your competition. Breaking bread together facilitates forging of an effective relationship.
- Taking opportunities, whether larger or small, for creative competition and collaboration.
- Challenging your competitor to resolve a conflict in a unique, daring, and fun way. It might just have a powerful impact on future interactions.
- Reading about leaders and leadership styles. Parse through the material and choose the pieces that best fit you. Assimilate these into your behavior to be the leader you most desire to work for.

You should never be proud of doing the right thing; you should just do it.
—Dean Smith, the former men's basketball
coach at the University of North Carolina

CHAPTER 2
Why Independent Physicians Matter

Shery

Physician independence matters. While health care cost, physician morale, and health of the community are reinforced where physician independence is strong, for Kelly and for me it was more than that. It was a calling, a drive so strong we were willing to set aside the natural competitiveness existing between two rival organizations and include other independent groups and the competing hospitals. Our vision was to truly focus on what was best for our community. Kelly and I know there is room for those physicians who desire hospital employment to work alongside those driven by independence. Yet, as we witnessed firsthand the effects of physicians shifting from independence to employment throughout our careers, we each grew stronger in our resolve that there is a better way. At our very core, Kelly and I each knew, long before we knew one another, that collaboration was the path to returning medical decision-making to those best trained to do so.

In the history of health care, physicians and hospitals have operated side by side in a symbiotic relationship. Each was independent from the other, each was dependent upon the other. A shift in this alignment began creeping into the industry about thirty years ago. At that time, health care was different. When a woman delivered a baby, she might expect to stay in the hospital a week. Primary care physicians were delivering many of those babies. Today, it is rare that the family physician delivers babies, and healthy moms and babies generally go home from the hospital within a day or two of delivery.

In the 1980s, the cost for health care was rising rapidly. Health maintenance organizations (HMOs) grew in popularity as they gave employers predictable costs for providing insurance. This was done by tightly controlling utilization. HMOs created closely managed networks of physicians and approved payment for service only if that service met criteria developed by their medical director, who was most likely located in another city or state. Physicians were held responsible for patient compliance and behavior. For those of us who understand the compliance frustrations of changing and maintaining our own positive diet, exercise, smoking, or alcohol behaviors, or who have attempted teaching a particular behavior out of a child, we can get a sense of how handicapped the physicians felt by these rules. HMOs often reclaimed physician payments if a patient stated that the physician had referred to an unapproved or out-of-network provider. Physicians felt the pressure of HMOs' utilization management diverting patients or delaying treatment, even as HMOs annually lowered provider reimbursement. Medicaid reduced provider reimbursement while increasing services that were required to be delivered. Medicare selectively reduced rates depending on the specialty. Physicians sought refuge in the safety of a large system that could stabilize their pay.

The 1980s were also the beginning of expanded growth of for-profit hospital networks, resulting in increased vulnerability of smaller not-for-profit institutions.[8] Multihospital systems were on the rise through hospital mergers and acquisitions. All this volatility created disequilibrium among physicians. As the hospital systems grew, they needed to ensure referrals to their facilities and services.

---

8 Barbra Mann Wall, "History of Hospitals," Nursing, History, and Health Care, University of Pennsylvania School of Nursing, accessed June 2021, https://www.nursing.upenn.edu/nhhc/nurses-institutions-caring/history-of-hospitals/.

Since the principal physician-patient relationship is with the primary-care provider, this was the first group to be recruited for hospital employment. As technology and pharmaceuticals improved, more of the medical hospital stays were eliminated, hospital and physician reimbursement decreased, and these patients were mostly managed through a medical specialist's office. Hospital rates for surgeries increased and became a primary revenue source for hospitals, resulting in greater recruitment of surgical specialists. This recruitment has accelerated in the last ten years to a level where more than half of the physicians in the US are now employed by hospital systems—although, this trend is starting to reverse.[9] However, it has been my observation that the majority of the specialties now offered through large, vertically integrated health systems called integrated delivery systems (IDSs), or "private equity," would better serve patients, employers, and the community by promoting and supporting independent providers. The reason is simple: cost of care to the purchaser of that care.

The 1990s saw continued health care cost escalation, with no relief in sight. This was a leading topic during my work meetings and conferences. I even studied it in graduate school and heard it all the time on the nightly news. Congress, under the influence of the strong and very well-funded hospital lobby, passed legislation based on the belief that physicians were the cause of the high medical costs. The thought was that if physicians own the service, they will over-refer to themselves, drive up the cost of care, and take advantage of patients. In came more and stronger regulations preventing physicians from self-referral, from working together to own and refer, while correspondingly increasing reporting requirements. Health care is now among the most highly regulated industries in America.

As regulations and reporting grew, infrastructure requirements increased. Centers for Medicare and Medicaid Services (CMS) agreed to offset some of the costs of these new information systems

---

9 Tanya Albert Henry, "Employed Physicians Now Exceed Those Who Own Their Practices," American Medical Association, posted May 10, 2019, https://www.ama-assn.org/about/research/employed-physicians-now-exceed-those-who-own-their-practices.

requirements, then attached even greater reporting requirements. There is no doubt that accountability for receiving money from the government is essential; however, the moving target of what would be paid and how to meet the goals set by CMS changed annually, sometimes retrospectively.

Adding further complexity to the system: all this movement by CMS created an opening for national insurance companies to institute similar quality criteria for payment and ranking. Note the word *similar*. Translation: each payer requires slightly different metrics for quality and cost reporting, increasing the burden of data collection and reporting. Payers then rank physicians and publish this to patients for health care decision-making. The information payers published was difficult to read, difficult to understand, and more difficult to validate, yet this data was shared publicly and used to rank the physicians. Once ranked, the physicians were categorized as "tier-one" or "tier-two" providers. With higher quality and lower costs, tier one placed the physician in a more prominent position on their website and would be the first physician offered if a patient called the health plan for a recommendation. Tier-two providers could be found buried within the website after some diligence and persistence.

Our physicians fared well on the quality ranking, which was a relief since patients reading the results could neither see nor, therefore, discern the background information, only whether the physician was a tier-one or tier-two provider. For a few of our physicians, cost was a different matter. We had a patient who moved to town in her eighth month of pregnancy. Prior to moving to town, this patient's previous physician ordered multiple expensive tests. Upon arriving to town, she established a patient-physician relationship with one of our obstetricians. The next month, she had a normal delivery and a healthy baby. Although our physician was not responsible for any of the expensive tests performed prior to her eighth month, the health plan's algorithm assigned all the costs to him and tagged him as an expensive provider. These management and cost burdens of reporting further push smaller practices toward the IDS, where they are promised a burden-free practice.

Attractive to the hospitals was the idea of vertical integration. If an IDS can own the entire supply chain, then the fear of losing business or maintaining the sometimes-thorny relationships with physicians becomes moot. When the hospital systems acquire physician practices, they also acquire the ancillary services and referrals of those practices. This means that upon employment, the revenue generating services previously performed in the physician offices, such as X-ray, lab, and physical therapy, are now performed by the hospital. This reduces market competition for those services, simultaneously increasing the purchaser's cost by 300 to 400 percent. This is because hospitals are paid significantly higher rates than physicians for the exact same services.[10]

Insurers are also complicit in the movement of physicians from private practice to employment. There is compression in physicians' reimbursement as the cost to run a practice and meet all the requisite-reporting requirements continues to rise. Payers are either holding reimbursement constant or decreasing payment to the providers. This produces confusion and conflicting messages for employers who are receiving health insurance renewal quotes that exceed what they expect based on their employees' use of medical services. Those increases are not flowing to the physicians, rather the additional cost improves return on investment for the insurers and their investors.

Physicians who want to stay independent are forced to find other revenue streams in the form of radiology, lab, surgery centers, and more. The benefit to us as consumers of health care services is that the cost is significantly less when performed at a physician-owned facility than at a hospital.

An example of an adverse effect of insurer interference happened in Indianapolis in the early 2000s. There were a number of freestanding (not hospital owned) imaging centers. During a meeting I attended with a large health-insurance company where several of these centers

---

10 Rand 3.0 Employer Hospital Price Transparency Project https://employerptp.org/.

were present, there was a plea from the imaging centers for a sustainable reimbursement that would still save the health plan that money. The reimbursement requested would allow freestanding centers to cover costs and reinvestment in plant and operations while still charging less than the hospitals. The pleas fell on deaf, albeit polite, ears, and the vast majority of centers sold to hospitals or went out of business. Today, most patients are paying three or four times more to have mammograms, MRIs, and other imaging services done at hospital-based imaging centers.

Another reason for keeping physicians independent is medical decision-making. The focus of business decision makers who are defending a bottom line is quite different from that of a physician whose focus is a patient's success. It is important to acknowledge that not all health systems and private-equity firms are solely financially focused, and not all physicians are properly patient focused. However, this is a generalization based on the reported experience of physicians and staff of health systems and equity partners.

According to Marni Jameson Carey in *Medical Economics*, "When hospitals or private equity groups buy up doctors, costs skyrocket, quality goes down, and if the hospital doing the acquiring is nonprofit, communities suffer financial harm because all the taxes that independent practice once paid come off the tax rolls."[11]

Physicians who are part of a system are told where to send their patients and to whom. Highly regarded independent physicians with long histories of supporting a hospital will lose referrals as soon as the system hires physicians of like specialty. This behavior chips away at the viability of the independent practice. It is not by mistake or by accident. Surgeons are pressured by hospitals to move to health systems. If the surgeon will not leave independent practice, the IDS simply brings a new physician into the area. Then additional pressure is levied through diverting referrals by the hospital-employed primary-care physicians, as instructed by hospital leadership, to the newly

11 Marni Jameson Carey, "Employed vs. Independent Doctors: Numbers Don't Tell the Whole Story," *Medical Economics*, June 5, 2019, https://www.medicaleconomics.com/view/employed-vs-independent-doctors-numbers-dont-tell-whole-story.

employed surgeon. Referrals to the independent surgeon occur less and less frequently as patients are sent to the surgeon employed by the hospital. Patients may have to wait months to see the employed doctor when they could be seen within days by an independent surgeon. We as patients are unknowingly forced to wait to receive services within the hospital system to ensure that all the revenue associated with that patient is captured by the hospital. The IDS pressures the independent physician by diverting patients, expecting that the physician will leave private practice to come where the referrals flow freely.

Over time, employers started demanding alternatives to the high cost of the hospital systems. These employers began engaging in medical tourism[12] in an effort to reduce costs. This, of course, has the unintended consequence of exacerbating increasing health-care costs in a community by further redirecting patients from independent providers.

There is no easy fix to the massively complex and multifaceted US health care system. We do, however, have the ability to undo some of the actions that are driving up costs and driving down quality. Organizations like Employers Forum of Indiana and the Advisory Board have been sounding the horns of change. A shared vision of building a better system that will benefit the entire community, rather than a few in the community, is what inspired us to collaborate and cooperate.

The passion Kelly and I both have for the benefits of physician independence was foundational to the strategies we each held for our groups. From our introductory meeting over breakfast in the fall of 2018 where we formed the basis of collaborative innovation, we forged a path toward strengthening physician independence.

Understand your health-care options:

---

12 Employers use medical tourism when they experience lower costs by sending an employee and family member outside the area to seek medical services.

- If you could pay $40,000 for a car or $4,000 for the exact same car with the same or higher level of service, which would you choose?
- Comparison shopping health services will net the highest quality at the best price.
- Engage your finance and HR decision makers to include provider options that will lower health-insurance costs, creating savings for the company.
- When you are being referred by your physician as you seek other services, ask, "To whom would you send your child/spouse/parent?"

Those who disrupt their industries change consumer behavior, alter economics, and transform lives.
—Heather Simmons, *Reinventing Dell*

CHAPTER 3
Was Rome Built in a Day?

Kelly

No, and health care won't be transformed in a day. However, disruptive change—change that really shifts how an industry interacts with its customers—can happen when the market is ripe, when consumers are demanding change, and others are willing to collaborate.

The health-care landscape in our market is much like that of the rest of the country. Health systems have continued to rapidly employ physicians while in some communities, the number of independent or community-based independent physician groups continues to decline or be eliminated altogether. In 2020, an American Medical Association survey showed the number of physicians employed by hospitals and health systems now exceeds the number of physicians in private practice.[13] The COVID-19 pandemic highlighted how vulnerable independent physician groups are when there are sudden, large decreases in outpatient visits, impacting revenue. Most independent physician practices are for-profit organizations and do not have access to the benefits of large for-profit hospital systems.

---

13 "AMA Analysis Shows Most Physicians Work Outside of Private Practice," Press Releases, American Medical Association, posted May 5, 2021, https://www.ama-assn.org/press-center/press-releases/ama-analysis-shows-most-physicians-work-outside-private-practice.

While independent physician groups have been shown to provide excellent quality at a lower cost, the economics of health care make it difficult to stay independent. Technology requirements, revenue-cycle infrastructure, lack of leverage with large payers, and competition in recruitment with larger organizations, among other factors, are all driving more and more community-based physicians to consider joining a health system. At the same time, employers are actively seeking options to lower health care expenses and provide more cost-effective benefit options for their employees. In a recent RAND study, Indiana ranked among the most expensive states in the country to receive health care.[14]

All these factors are creating an environment where the right stakeholders can disrupt the status quo and bring value to patients, employers, and the community. This is precisely what I see happening in our market.

Shery and I connected shortly after I came to Indiana. In my first few weeks in my new role, I had several people ask me if I had met Shery yet. So I looked her up on LinkedIn and we met for breakfast. That breakfast meeting was like a meeting among old friends. We could have talked all day. We left that meeting with so many ideas and had a plan to meet again. I had spent the last fifteen years in Minnesota, leading population health and ambulatory care, and was looking for a new challenge where I could bring value to the physicians I support as well as to the community, and bring meaningful change. When I came to interview and meet the physicians, it was clear to me they had a vision and a mission I wanted to be a part of. I knew that together, Shery and I would bring something new and meaningful to our market.

I think back to our first meeting often. We met at a popular breakfast spot where many local business leaders meet. Although we did not know each other, we jumped right into the issues our organizations

---

14 "Hospital Price Comparisons in Indiana," RAND Health Care, RAND Corporation, n.d., https://www.rand.org/health-care/projects/price-transparency/hospital-pricing/indiana-hospital-prices.html.

were facing and it felt like we had known each other for twenty years. The local health systems were continuing to recruit our physicians or replace our surgeons with their own employed doctors. While we were working hard to recruit and grow our practices, it was difficult to compete with the guaranteed salaries the health systems offered to physicians. Declining reimbursement and increasing overhead were also impacting the economics of the independent medical groups. We both saw these factors and the reality that if we did not find a way to support the region's independent-physician groups, many of these practices would not remain financially viable and ultimately be purchased by a local health system or simply close their doors. While communities need the valuable inpatient and emergency services provided by a hospital system, outpatient services are less expensive when provided by independent-physician practices as they don't charge additional facility fees for imaging, infusions, and outpatient surgery. Health-insurance companies also reimburse hospital systems much more for the same procedures and office visits independent physician practices provide in a lower-cost care setting. We recognized it would not be an easy task, but taking no action would likely result in the independent-physician-practice model of care going away over the next several years and health care costs continuing to rise. We began to plan.

First on the list was to pull together like-minded physician practice leaders from around the region. We spent a few months meeting with physician-practice leaders in the area to listen and better understand their challenges as well as to gauge their interest in coming together to tackle the issues impacting this model of care. Our goal was to create a network in which we could support each other and a mission to preserve the independent-physician care model, and create a value proposition for employers in the region. Eventually, we created Paramount Care Group, LLC, (PCG) which was officially launched in August 2019 with four original partners as the foundation of the network. PCG launched with two hundred providers and has continued to grow to three hundred providers as of this book's publication. Interest from the broker and employer community has been tremendous as they were searching for networks and new, innovative services that would assist their clients in reducing their health care spend for their employees. We now have direct contracts with employers, and we are working with surgical-bundling companies to create lower-cost, bundled service agreements for common surgical procedures. We are also beginning discussions with payers to look at opportunities in value-based care contracts, where we have an opportunity to share in the savings created if we are able to reduce the cost of care for attributed patients.

A part of the strategy for preserving independence for physician practices includes assessing opportunities for growth that lessen independence on the health systems for revenue and shift appropriate care to lower-cost-of-care settings. For example, many of our surgeons participate in the trauma service and support for the local hospitals. The hospitals need this coverage to provide care for the community but also to meet regulatory requirements. As they employ their own physician staff and replace the independent doctors that have been providing these services in their facilities for decades, our physicians lose this revenue. We assessed opportunities to grow our own ambulatory care networks that can provide lower-cost outpatient services and looked for gaps or services we do not currently provide for the community. We created an aggressive growth plan and added new services to support the community, including a breast center, a sleep center, and a bariatric program; grew the types of procedures we can provide in our ambulatory surgery center or in office settings; and added a second immediate care center as well as new imaging services. All of these services would expand access to care and are provided in care settings that are low cost. An opportunity to invest in a physician-owned medical and surgical hospital came to us in early 2019, and we began to assess this opportunity with an expanded group of independent physicians. These physician groups had been fierce competitors for years, but they understood we were all facing similar challenges, including being slowly replaced by the hospital systems. It took some time to build enough trust to consider coinvesting as owners of this hospital.

After close to a year of intense due diligence, three local physician practices came together and invested in what is now Concordance Hospital, a twenty-nine bed hospital with four operating rooms and two procedure rooms with plenty of opportunity to grow. The vision of this collaboration was to create a physician-led and -owned inpatient and outpatient facility where doctors could drive both the clinical and patient experience. In traditional hospital systems, most care-delivery decisions are not made by physicians. Physicians may have input, but often nonphysicians are driving patient experience and quality-improvement initiatives and strategies to improve patient care. A model where physicians own and lead clinical-care decisions and ensure collaboration and continuity postdischarge increases overall quality of care. Concordance Hospital would join the Paramount Care Group network, and we would reduce the cost of surgeries through bundled-pricing initiatives. This collaboration of three independent physician groups that have competed for years is a rare event.

As exciting as we saw this collaboration, it was not seen as a positive step by our hospital-system partners. Rather, it was seen as an aggressive competitive move and was met with a significant reaction. Physicians who would provide care at Concordance received threats. They were essentially given an ultimatum: either pull out of the investment at Concordance or the hospital system would pull the trigger on what they described as their "nuclear option," including the elimination of any and all contracts in which physicians benefited from financially, immediate termination of these physicians from leadership positions at the health system, and a promise to aggressively compete. Their use of the term "nuclear" was intended to intimidate and pressure us into not following through with the investment. Although Concordance Hospital is a small fraction of the size of the local hospital systems, and despite our efforts to highlight that this investment would have little-to-no impact on their volumes, they did not back down on their threats. Large hospital systems have access to revenues independent physician groups do not. They are often not-for-profit organizations and can take advantage of tax breaks and other financial benefits.

As mentioned earlier, with their size comes leverage with payer reimbursement and much higher reimbursement from insurance companies. All of these factors make it difficult to compete with and stand up to these organizations.

Obviously, these threats were not taken lightly by any of the physicians involved. The doctors have watched the health system replace them for years and saw the writing on the wall, but at the same time, they worried about how they would replace the revenue they would lose if the health system followed through with their "nuclear option." After much discussion, they decided to move ahead with a strategy they believed would preserve their independence and close on the investment at Concordance. Immediately, the local health system followed through on all of its threats. Out of the three physician groups invested in Concordance, all the physicians were removed from and no longer allowed to participate on that hospital system's committees, be in any leadership positions, and so on. Our fifteen OB-GYNs, who provided labor support, were replaced with physicians from outside the community, and most of the on-call-related contracts were eliminated. This hospital system had canceled each contract couriered, and for an added special touch, they had each canceled agreement hand-delivered to me, which I perceived as another intimidation tactic. Despite everything that happened, we remained committed to our mission to preserve this independent model of care and maintain alternative, high-quality, cost-effective care for the communities we serve.

Through both of these major initiatives, it became clear that two of the physician groups shared many common interests, including the absolute mission to preserve health care choice in our communities. Both groups were working on very similar strategies to stay viable despite all the market forces actively working to drive them out of business. Shery and I met with our physician leaders and discussed how we could bring our practices together. We believed we would be stronger together as we faced the actions of the hospital system. Our two groups began merger conversations, and soon both partnerships voted to officially merge. Throughout the due diligence process, we sought advice from other independent groups that had faced similar challenges. One group from the Chicago area came and shared insights with our physicians about their journey of growth and bringing together like-minded physician groups. In June 2020, in the middle of the global pandemic, the River Valley Care Providers and MidAmerica Specialists officially merged.

So, in less than two years, we launched Paramount Care Group, invested in Concordance Hospital, and successfully navigated a merger of two highly respected organizations with very deep histories in the community. When we began each of these initiatives, we did not know how or if they would come together or even be successful. There were strategies that would require very intentional work to get these physician groups to communicate, work together, and build trust.

These changes brought disruption to the market in a way we hope will change the status quo and trajectory of health care in this region. Together, we can work to support the community, provide exceptional care, and bring down the cost of care. Our hope is that, with time, the health systems will see there is room for all of us and that the community needs independent providers just as much as it needs the hospitals.

There has been so much learning in the past two years for us, our physicians, and, I believe, our larger communities. We have seen the absolute best of partnership and collaboration and the worst in negative forces committed to derailing our efforts. One of the most exciting times for me was at a joint-partner meeting between River Valley Care Partners and MidAmerica Specialists. It was so great to see these two incredibly well-respected physician groups and longtime competitors in the same room, sharing dinner and talking about the value of our organizations working together. They were all facing the same issues and worried about the fate of their independent practices as the hospital system's actions threatened their existence. I also watched a hospital set in motion a series of actions that were intended to financially devastate these community-based physicians who have been providing care in their hospital for decades for the sole reason they dared to compete and try to keep their practices financially viable. Having worked in hospital systems for more than twenty years, I had never seen anything like this before. In my previous health system leadership roles, I worked hard to maintain good relationships with the independent-physician groups because I knew that our working together was mutually beneficial. We wanted their admissions and inpatient support, and they needed a place to provide care for their patients. There were times we competed and times we worked together, but we always found common ground to support each other for the benefit of the community.

The actions taken by the hospital systems in our market have only deepened the resolve of the independent groups. They know they provide value to their community, and their existence ensures choice and high-quality, cost-effective care. They are more committed than ever to this mission.

A few thoughts for consideration:

- Fight for change that is meaningful and brings value.
- This type of disruptive change brings risks, so do an exhaustive review of the risks and benefits but know that you might not succeed in early phases of disruptive change.
- There will be pushback, maybe significant pushback. Be ready, prepare your teams, and stay consistent in messaging about the value proposition of the work.

The rest of this book is dedicated to sharing what we experienced as we challenged the status quo and how we managed every barrier that got in our way.

Optimism is the faith that leads to achievement.
Nothing can be done without hope and confidence.
—Helen Keller

CHAPTER 4
Delusional Optimism

Kelly

Optimism, it seems, is partly genetic, partly learned, and a bit environmental.[15] Regardless of any studies or one's opinion on the matter, adverse circumstances and experiences rarely leave us unchanged. There is a quote I love that may have first been attributed to Nancy Reagan: "Human beings are like tea bags. You can't tell how strong we are until we are put in hot water."[16]

Where we find that adversity has shaped us into a better version of ourselves is also where we find the incubation of our superpower. It is where we find leaders who have reprioritized what is meaningful and redefined success—through optimism. It *is* a choice.

Recently, after reading an update I had sent to the partnership about our financials and a few organizational changes, one of the physicians I work with said, "Kelly, you are always the optimist!"

---

15 Denise Mann, "Optimism May Be Partly in Your Genes: Researchers Zero in on Optimism, Self-esteem Gene," Health and Balance, WebMD, reviewed September 16, 2011, https://www. webmd.com/balance/news/20110916/optimism-partly-in-your-genes#1.

16 "Nancy Reagan Quotes," QuoteFancy, n.d., https://quotefancy.com/quote/1379164/Nancy-Reagan-A-woman-is-like-a-tea-bag-She-only-knows-her-strength-when-put-in-hot-water#:~:text=Nancy%20Reagan%20Quote%3A%20%E2%80%9CA%20woman,when%20put%20in%20hot%20water.%E2%80%9D.

There is a balance in ensuring full transparency but also communicating hope. In this particular update, I ended my note with "Our future is bright" because I genuinely believe this to be true. Honestly, I could not tell if his reply was a compliment or not, but often my optimism is met with skepticism.

So I responded respectfully, though with my usual level of sarcasm: "Well, someone has to be!"

Wikipedia defines the word *optimism* as "an attitude reflecting a belief or hope that the outcome of some specific endeavor, or outcomes in general, will be positive, favorable, and desirable."[17] I think that essentially describes my outlook in general despite many life circumstances that could have just as easily turned me into a pessimist. Is optimism a bad quality? Some see my optimism toward projects or initiatives as unrealistic or think my expectations are set too high. I appreciate this viewpoint, and it has pushed me to examine my thoughts more and to be sure I'm setting realistic goals and expectations not only for myself but for my teams. My approach has never been to aim low, which is likely a good thing as the leader of an organization. I aim high and work hard to achieve the set targets. At my roots, I know that I adopted this trait after a series of very difficult life challenges when I was a young single mom. It was a choice for me—I chose, against all odds, to succeed for my children and my family. I now also choose optimism for the success of the company I have the privilege to lead, the team members I have the opportunity to support, and the community we provide care for.

My professional journey to the seat of CEO has been a little less than normal, but I think it makes me even more grateful for the honor to support and lead. The difficult life challenges I referenced relate to my personal journey. I grew up with every advantage a kid could have. My dad was a cardiologist, and he certainly blessed me and my family with opportunities to travel, taught us the value of education and music, and, most importantly, always expressed his love for us. My

---

17 Wikipedia, "Optimism," Wikipedia, Free Encyclopedia, updated November 24, 2021, https://en.wikipedia.org/wiki/Optimism.

mom stayed home with us for many years, and from her unrelenting support, I learned how to be a mother myself. Honestly, how much better can it get? I have five incredibly talented siblings, three brothers and two sisters—yes, a bit like *The Brady Bunch*. With great parents and all this support, how could anything go wrong?

Turns out, through my own choices.

As a senior in high school, I had big plans. I was a cheerleader and an all-state sprinter on our track team who planned to run in college and eventually go to medical school. I found out I was pregnant at seventeen years old. Not part of my "big plans." My parents reacted how you might expect. My dad was deeply disappointed. My mother, who had raised us in the Catholic Church, was also incredibly disappointed but said she would support me—although I am quite sure she never really recovered. Literally, thereafter, my mom would introduce me and then say, "She got pregnant in high school but is doing okay now."

Despite my parents concerns, I did what I believed was right and became a mom. I also married my then-boyfriend, Max. When I graduated from high school at eighteen years old, I was married and six months pregnant. At my graduation, I was voted most athletic and most accident-prone. True story. It's helpful to have a good sense of humor.

It was the night I got married that I experienced domestic violence for the first time, and as I think back to that night, I cannot even remember what led to it. We were in the car driving to Detroit and arguing, and then he hit me in the arm, very hard. It was almost like a switch was turned on. He was someone I no longer really knew. As if it were yesterday, I remember sitting there in our old red Buick car after this episode of violence and really feeling the full weight of the situation I was in, but with no idea at all what to do about it.

As I have reflected over the years, it became clear that our marriage was not what he had wanted. We both were from very religious families, and I am sure he felt pressured to "do the right thing" and get married, which led to resentment. My sadness triggered his anger even more, and his need for control increased.

For me, it was different. I was incredibly stubborn and wanted to prove to my parents I could be successful and that this marriage could work. Before that night, I had never experienced or been exposed to domestic violence, so I responded like the textbook definition of a battered woman. I made excuses for his behavior and believed it was my fault. I was eighteen and had no understanding of what was happening. I didn't tell anyone about this, but as time went on, I know family and friends grew suspicious.

Those who know me well know I am incredibly tenacious and slightly stubborn—well, maybe more than slightly. I was determined to show my family and community I could be a mom and still achieve all my goals. Nicole Christine was born on September 9, 1983, and was more beautiful than I could have imagined. One of the nurses on the maternity floor kept saying to me, "You're just a baby having a baby."

My maternal instincts kicked in pretty quickly after having my first child, and while I was terrified most of the time, my mom and mother-in-law taught me so much. In a weird coincidence, they both happened to be named Judy, yet these two Judys could not be more different. We lived in a house on the family farm, so I had a garden and learned how to can and freeze vegetables.

Then, Brendan Michael was born in 1985, and Natalie Elizabeth was born in 1988.

Shortly after Brendan was born, I enrolled in classes and, eventually, the nursing program as I saw this as a good starting point to what I thought would be a slightly delayed entry into medical school. My husband did not like my going to school. He had an ideal image of me being like the mother figures from his own childhood, which were stay-at-home moms. He also couldn't control me when I was away from home. When I returned from classes or even from a visit to my parents' house, he would search my bags and take any money he found.

The violence at home continued. I worked very hard to keep it secret, but I know the people closest to me could see my husband's behavior and the impact it had on me. I was in a constant state of anxiety. Most days, I would spend a few hours with my mom to get out of the house.

And almost within the minute I got there, the phone would ring. Max wanted to know when I was coming home. If I stayed for a range of time he deemed too long, he would show up to take me home.

Then my youngest daughter, Brittany Lee, was born on September 9, 1988, several weeks early and with significant health issues. Brittany aspirated at the delivery and ultimately was flown to a specialty NICU in Ohio for ECMO, a heart and lung bypass that would allow her lungs to rest and heal. Brittany developed other serious health issues, including gastrointestinal (GI) problems that would require a bowel transplant. She spent several months in the NICU and came home on oxygen. Brittany was clearly happy to be home and jumped right into being the little sister. Despite many more hospital stays, she was just one of the kids when she was home, and I knew that she loved being home more than anything. She was silly, played with her sisters and brother, and loved watching *The Little Mermaid*. We spent the next two years trying to understand Brittany's GI issues that caused countless episodes of sepsis and hospital stays. We traveled to specialists across the country for answers, and ultimately the only option became a bowel transplant, which was experimental and came with a very low likelihood of survival. We made the difficult decision to take her home and not pursue the surgery. Brittany Lee passed away at home on March 23, 1991. Her death is still surreal, even as I write this today.

During the almost-three years of Brittany's life, the difficulties at home only escalated. My time away from home, around others who made me feel like I was smart, improved my confidence, and Max could see that. I developed friendships with other moms with sick children and saw that my life was not normal. I also saw it in their eyes when they observed some of his controlling behaviors. Brittany's life, in some ways, brought me back to who I really am, and I knew that to protect the lives of my other children, I needed to leave. I sought help from a local YWCA program, and for the first time, I met other women like me. The YWCA had a class I attended where they walked through the cycle of violence. I was sitting in this classroom in a folding chair with a few other women while they described to me exactly what was happening in my house. Many of the other women had spouses who were alcoholics or drug users. My situation was different, though, in that none of those particular stereotypes applied.

It was that day I made a plan to leave. I began to save money. I hid it in a blue tin can in a white antique cupboard in my basement. I wanted to be sure I had enough money to rent an apartment and cover car payments until I could get on my feet. I was cleaning houses and mowing lawns to save as much money as I could.

On one particularly tough night, Max and I had an argument that escalated to a situation in which he threatened to take his own life. We were all in the kitchen at 3:00 a.m., and I was holding two of the kids with the third wrapped around my thigh. Instantly, I thought to myself: *We are done tonight.* I loaded up my beautiful babies, and we left.

There was a lot of risk in leaving, but to ensure the best life for my children, I needed to fight for them. We took off with a few clothes and the money I had been saving. I remember counting six hundred dollars, which seemed like a million to me at the time. I was also blessed to have an extended family who would be there for me and my kids.

I learned so much from Brittany's short life. She taught me how to be strong and confident so that, whatever happened next, I could provide the best life for my children. She also opened my eyes to a whole new world of health care I had no idea existed. I watched families be treated differently because they were on Medicaid and also watched families with chronically ill children have to sell their homes and belongings to pay for medications. I experienced health care as a true patient versus a doctor's daughter who never had to worry about the cost of an office visit or, God forbid, an emergency helicopter ride. The other lessons came from my three older children who have grown into amazing adults. Two have had military careers, and one is an incredible leader in health care. They are really special humans who don't use what happened to them as a crutch or an excuse. I became stronger from their love and strength.

A friend from nursing school introduced me to Daren, and a year and a half later, we married. Together, we worked then and continue to work now to provide a healthy and safe home for our family.

Max did not go away quietly, as you might imagine. What I feared and what kept me from leaving for eight years became very real. He made it his mission in life to take the kids from me. Finally, after a psychological evaluation, the court was provided with a picture of the risk my kids and I were facing. Even then, the court allowed supervised visitation with his own mother as the supervisor. The court also provided an avenue for him to get professional help, and he could petition the court for visits, but he never followed through. Max was eventually convicted of felony aggravated stalking and assault. When we were certain he was out of our lives, Daren and I left the state to get a fresh start.

At this point, you likely have a pretty clear picture why my professional journey did not have the typical start. I stayed in school, worked as a realtor, and eventually took a position as a medical-practice manager. I fell in love with this work, supporting providers and physicians. While I loved the patient care I experienced in nursing, through my experiences with Brittany's life, I believed I could have more of an impact supporting physicians and transforming the patient experience as well.

I worked my way up through various positions. I scheduled patients, learned about electronic medical records (EMRs), and became a certified EMR trainer. I led revenue-cycle work and the financial end of the business of health care. I received my bachelor's degree the same year my daughter turned eighteen and graduated from high school. I earned my master's degree a few years later. While I loved the work, leading physician practices, I kept pushing myself to take roles that would allow me a different seat at the table, a seat where I could help drive meaningful change. Change that actually made the delivery of care better and easier. I had this fire inside to take what I learned while trying to navigate health care for my daughter and work to improve the patient experience. I was fortunate to earn various executive positions in large health systems and so grateful for those opportunities to learn about the business of corporate health care. All these incredibly difficult and some painful experiences led me to where I am today. My own life experiences have taught me I can literally accomplish anything, and most things are possible if you start from a place of yes. When I first joined River Valley Care Providers, we had a strategic-planning session aimed at developing a plan that would help the company grow and remain viable for years to come. With the physicians and executive leaders, we assessed opportunities to replace revenues lost from local hospitals who were replacing the community-based physicians. I asked the question: What if we had ownership in a hospital? Yes, why *not*? While owning a hospital was a big undertaking, we had to start somewhere and help with the issue of lost revenue. There were other values in owning a hospital, including the opportunity to reduce the cost of care for expensive inpatient and outpatient medical and surgical stays as well as provide an exceptional patient experience. Physicians owning a hospital would also lead to clinical and quality improvements as well. We started with saying yes to the idea, and the work to make it happen began.

Rarely does everything go according to plan. There are adjustments and modifications throughout. Buying or investing in a hospital, for example, came with a few bumps. The local health-system reaction to this investment was significant and not in a positive way. They took this investment as a threat and responded accordingly, taking away any remaining contracts or physician leadership roles. There was also significant work to do in the hospital's clinical structure so it would be ready to care for medical patients. We closed on the hospital investment in February 2020, and less than thirty days later, the first wave of COVID-19 hit, and elective surgical cases were stopped. I am not sure our timing could have been any worse. All these "bumps" caused us to more than once reconsider our plan. At the end of the day, we pushed forward to accomplish our goal.

When a leader is open to what is possible, it is easier to work through the issues that come along. With the hospital and everything that went wrong, we had plenty of reasons to just walk away. I had one full day when COVID-19 hit, and I thought, *My God, what have we done?* I was at the hospital with the leadership team when the governor's mandate to stop all elective cases came out in a press release. My cell phone started buzzing with dozens of texts from physicians and staff asking if I had seen the news. I quickly pulled myself together and came up with a financial plan to reduce costs and help get the organization through this ordeal. We have taken on every challenge one at a time and moved past them. What I've learned is that if I have an open mind and an open heart to whatever comes my direction, amazing opportunities will come. On occasion, doors will shut, but I will remain open to seeing the possibilities.

As I said, I do believe optimism is a choice. We can choose to see the opportunities in front of us and believe we can make them a reality, or we can choose to see all the obstacles that could cause failure. Over the years, I have come to realize that some people are not wired to see "what could be," and when offered an opportunity or a proposal for a new venture or project, they quickly begin listing all the reasons why it won't work or what might ultimately go wrong.

The investment in the hospital was a perfect showcase for optimism as a choice. We had some physicians who were concerned that the current model for anesthesia was not safe. My response to them was that we would change the model and create a new physician-led anesthesia program. They had doubt we could get this new model launched, but, today, we have a new physician-led anesthesia program. The existing model was a barrier, so we came up with a plan and removed the barrier. During the first wave of COVID-19, the leadership team was faced with declining volumes and an expense infrastructure the financials could not support. We needed a plan to ramp down expenses as volume declined and ramp back up when things improved. I asked the team for a plan that would reduce monthly expenses by $2 million dollars. I quickly heard, "That is not possible."

My response was, "Yes, it is, and I will help you do it."

Initially, the conversation circled around what we couldn't do: change all the vendors and contracts that could *not* be changed. So we took it day by day, contacted our vendors and suppliers, and worked out creative plans to accomplish our financial target. The team faced incredibly hard decisions about how to reduce staffing hours to meet business needs, knowing the painful impact it would have on our teams. We shifted our focus to creating a plan that would allow the business to survive so our staff would have a business to return to. None of this was easy, and the impact to our organization was and continues to be tremendous, but I believe the team learned what is possible when we shift our thinking from what we can't do to what we *can* do.

I've come to learn that my eternally optimistic "yes, we can" approach can be a little scary to my colleagues and more than a little annoying to my kids. Once in a while, when my kids were younger, they would remind me that sometimes they didn't need a pep talk with a positive spin about something bad that happened at school. They just needed a hug from their mom and acknowledgment that whatever it was that happened did indeed just suck. So, on occasion, I keep my optimism to myself. With my team, I can see where my constant "sure, we can do that" attitude scares the heck out of them. Quite honestly, saying no is easier.

One day, my CFO and I were on a call negotiating our ownership interest in the hospital-facility real estate. One of the other investor groups had been vocal about how they expected to be the primary owners of the facility, so I knew we would have to be assertive to get the ownership level we wanted. We hadn't had a chance to prep before the call, so when I said on the call that we expected to have majority interest in the facility, which was a much bigger investment than we really intended on making, I could literally feel her anxiety through the phone! I really expected us to just have equal-ownership share, but my style is to put it out there, knowing we will hopefully land where we need to. Fortunately, it somehow all worked out, and we ended up with the exact ownership level we wanted.

Another time, Shery and I were in a meeting with a CEO from one of the local health systems. We sat side by side with this CEO sitting across the table from us as we discussed some opportunities to create a management service organization, the details of what board representation might look like, and many other very boring details. This CEO pushed for a board seat, and I simply said, "Sure, why not? We can work that out."

I couldn't see Shery's face from where I was sitting, but I'm quite sure I thought she was going to fall out of her chair. We had specifically talked about this exact scenario and the importance of limiting this organization's board representation. In the moment, my "sure" attitude got us past the part of the discussion that revolved around ego and the need for control, and to the important details of the collaboration. I was not disingenuous in my response but simply agreed to work through governance once we got to the most important part of the discussion, which was: *Are we going to collaborate at all?* I have learned that some pre-meeting prep can help my colleagues better understand my approach to saying sure most of the time. It simply allows the conversation to continue. Sometimes it advances, and sometimes it doesn't, but at least we did not limit ourselves right out of the gate over a board seat that may never come to fruition.

For me, career success is rooted in my optimistic "yes" approach. When I think about some of the amazing collaborations I've experienced, a few lessons come to mind:

- Take the breakfast meeting, lunch, or call. Just start with yes, then listen and learn. It may take time for the seed to bring forth fruit, but it's a start. This is not easy for introverts like me to do, but it is worth the investment.
- Surround yourself with other collaborators with a similar approach and willingness to see what's possible. This is exactly why Shery and I work so well together, even if my approach to yes may scare her a time or two. Two leaders with a no-boundaries approach to what's possible can accomplish just about anything!

- Listen to the negativity or naysayers, but don't let it deter you. There will be plenty of people who will offer their advice or thoughts about why your plans or new ventures will not work. Stay positive and keep moving forward.
- At times, the intensity of initiatives, or even the number of initiatives, can cause some trepidation. Do it anyway. Put it all out there and see what sticks. The payoff is worth the risk.

A woman with a voice is by definition a strong woman.
But the search to find that voice can be remarkably difficult.
—MELINDA GATES

CHAPTER 5
The Value of Diversity

Kelly

Through the work, Shery and I started to change our local health care landscape, and we encountered, as you might imagine, some resistance to collaboration and change. What we experienced initially was what I would describe as simply not being taken seriously. Why? I believe part of it was that we are female leaders in a very male-dominated health care leadership community. Some might call it a "good ol' boys' club."

I remember the first meeting we had with a local health care CEO. We were making rounds with leaders to let them know about one of our major initiatives to launch a clinically integrated network to support independent physician groups. Out of everything we were working on, we believed this initiative could be the most disruptive as the health systems might see this as competing with their own networks. This health care leader listened, metaphorically patted us on the heads, and then sent us on our way. He was very polite, smiled and nodded a lot, said he'd think about how they could participate.

As we departed, he said, "Well, good for you."

He clearly did not see the effort as serious on any level. As we walked away, I wondered if that conversation would have gone differently had we been one of his male competitors. I believe the answer is yes.

According to healthcaredive.com, 18 percent of health-care CEOs are female and 82 percent are male in an industry where 65 percent of the workforce is female.[18] Why is this? I think the answer is fairly complex. There are a number of factors that I believe inhibit women from being promoted to senior leadership roles. One that I have experienced personally is the perception of what a "strong leader" acts and looks like. Any notion that you can be an exceptional leader and yet somehow empathetic and supportive is not encouraged in many corporate cultures. In a previous C-suite role, the CEO I reported to would refer to me as a "mama bear." This topic would come up in our one-on-one sessions. He would describe me as a "great collaborator"—not meant to be a compliment, as he thought I was too soft with my team and invested more time on team building and development, which was viewed as soft or weak. Our leadership styles were very different.

Often, the loudest, most dominating person in the room is perceived as a strong leader. In this same organization, the C-suite was referred to as a "shark tank," and being strong and assertive was an absolute requirement for survival. I was one of two women at the senior-leader table, and we often endured listening to our male counterparts using inappropriate references you might hear in a bar. After a late board meeting, a few board members and executive team members met for a brief happy hour. One of the board members began telling stories openly about the prenuptial agreement he got his wife to sign.

Then my boss caught my eye and said, "We probably should not be talking about this in front of you, right?"

My response to him was, "Right—or, really, you shouldn't talk about this in front of anyone."

There were countless afternoons where the male C-suite members would go golfing together while the female leaders stayed in the office. I was actually invited to a local CEO group by a physician executive,

---

18 Marisa Torrieri, "Why Women Account for Just a Fraction of Hospital CEOs," Hospitals, *HealthCare Dive*, published December 1, 2014, https://www.healthcaredive.com/news/why-women-account-for-just-a-fraction-of-hospital-ceos/337822/.

but he quickly uninvited me by saying, "Oh, I'm sorry, it's really only men that come to that meeting."

The boys' club is alive and well.

One of the funniest examples of this "boys-only" culture was when a physician I work with stopped by to let me know he thought I was doing a good job. He said that if I ever needed him to "get some of my deals done," I could just let him know and he'd help me out by taking some of these guys to the bar because "that's where the real work typically happens."

I politely thanked him for his offer and told him that in my nearly thirty years of work in health care, I've never needed to "meet the boys at the bar" in order to get a deal done.

Another physician shared with me, in what I believe was intended to be a compliment, that I had the strongest maternal instinct he had ever seen in a leader. I was momentarily very confused. How could my role as CEO and my maternal instincts cross paths? I asked him if he believed that he perceived all the physicians as though they were my children. Do men lead with their paternal instincts? Does anyone ever tell a male leader they have strong paternal instincts? Simply: no.

Strong female leaders are still often seen as aggressive. In my first VP role, I received feedback that one of my male counterparts on the executive team thought I was a "bitch." I hate that word. I was driving home from work when I answered a call from my boss, Dan. He shared that his colleague thought I was a bitch because I was too pushy. I told him I could not believe he shared that with me, and that I hoped he provided feedback to this leader about how inappropriate this was in describing a female colleague. I was so angry and hurt, I went home, sat on my deck, and cried. I thought of my daughters, and I hoped that by the time they finished their education and went into the workforce, we would be in a different world where women are seen as equals in leadership and the use of this type of language and behavior would be gone.

I do believe that some of this behavior is driven by the competitive nature that exists in any corporate environment; nonetheless, we have some more work to do.

It is important to note that I've also been blessed to work with many outstanding male leaders. One physician leader I worked with in Minnesota is a person I'm honored to know, and I've personally learned a great deal from him. As a leader and a person, he is the very picture of respect. He is the very description of servant leadership. I had the opportunity to watch him coach very complex situations with calmness and grace. The area I learned the most from him was how he created boundaries around his work schedule and had such a great focus on what was important or created value. He is an essentialist— one of my now-favorite books he shared with me is *Essentialism* by Greg McKoewn. He managed his calendar around organizational and personal priorities. If a meeting did not help achieve a professional priority, he would decline the meeting. I, on the other hand, accepted every meeting to be sure I didn't miss out on an opportunity or offend anyone. The result was twelve hours of meetings per day and the feeling as though I was accomplishing nothing. I am still working hard to become an essentialist and prioritize my schedule and my work. This leader also taught me to see how important alignment of values is with the organization we work for. Seems so simple, and yet ...

Once, during an executive meeting, some of the language around the table became inappropriate. He knew I had been struggling with some of the unprofessional and disrespectful behaviors displayed by organizational leaders. During this meeting, he simply texted me the words "values mismatch."

Up to the time of that text message, I thought the reason I was struggling with the behavior of my peers and fitting in was my issue, that I needed to adjust or toughen up versus the possibility that this culture was simply not a match for my values. *Boom.* Mind blown.

This was a great learning experience for me. I stopped beating myself up and, instead, began looking at these situations differently. I am eternally grateful for the influence this physician has had on my career and for being such a good friend.

★★★

I am currently so blessed to lead and work with an amazing executive team. This is a team I inherited in part and added to through a merger. My team is mostly female, but that was not intentional. Still, I am a strong believer in the value of diversity. What's interesting is the feedback I get for not having more male leaders on my team when I've spent an entire career almost always as the sole woman at the table.

Many employees have come into my office and asked me if I minded sharing how I felt about having a mostly female executive team. I shared I hadn't thought about the team as male or female, just that we have the right leaders at the table. During the years I was one of the few female leaders at the table, not one person ever asked me what I thought about the fact that these teams were predominantly made up of men.

What can we do to reduce the impact of gender when trying to collaborate? When I think about the successes of the collaboration I have experienced in the last few years of my career, specifically working with Shery, I realize it all happened because there was no ego, power struggles, or turf battles involved, just leaders willing to work together for the common good of the community. There's been no bravado, grandstanding, or bullying to try to get the upper hand, just a common interest to bring meaningful change that would benefit our organizations and the larger community. I was so fortunate to find other leaders in the community who shared a similar vision and interest in seeing what we could do together versus the need to dominate and compete. When Shery and I began discussing our two organizations merging, we strongly felt that we both wanted what was best for the future of our organizations as well as the future of health care in our communities. Our roles and titles would not be the focus. We joked about arm wrestling over the CEO position. I'm pretty sure we both won.

How do you face leading significant or disruptive changes knowing you may experience these types of behaviors? I've had the great fortune to serve as a mentor to women who are earlier in their careers, and my best advice to these female leaders always includes:

- Work on your confidence. A great book I always recommend is *You Are a Badass: How to Stop Doubting Your Greatness* by Jen Sincero. The book is really funny and a great way to remind yourself just how amazing you are!
- You can be a strong leader *and* be caring and empathetic. These are the strengths of good leaders, not weaknesses.
- Don't be bullied. Always stand up for yourself and do not accept inappropriate or demeaning behavior. Walk away when you need to.
- Find a leadership group. This is a great way to build a network of other leaders all dealing with the same issues.
- Find a mentor. You may find one in the leadership group, or you may find one in your own organization who is willing to provide feedback to you and help you grow and develop.
- Find a sponsor within your organization that can help get you exposure within the company and assist with growth opportunities within the organization.
- Let your teams see you as a human. People want to see you as a real person.
- Manage your emotions. I'm not much of a crier, but I remember being so angry once, I thought I'd burst into tears right in front of everyone during a meeting. Excuse yourself from the situation and take a moment.
- Stop being everyone's caretaker. You don't need to be the last one in a meeting room to clean up or make sure everyone has water. These are nonpromotable tasks. Do your male counterparts do this? No, they do not. This was something I was doing and had no idea until an executive coach working with a team I was on pointed it out. For some reason, I felt compelled to make sure everything was set up for meetings, and I'd clean up after the meeting ended. This behavior will not serve you well.
- Male leaders, pay attention to your own gender biases. Do you depend on female colleagues to take notes in a meeting

or clean up after the board meeting? If so, this is your opportunity to make some changes! Work with an executive coach. Having an objective person help you continue growing and developing as a leader is priceless.

No rational argument will have a rational effect
on a man who does not want to adopt a rational attitude.
—KARL POPPER, AUSTRIAN BRITISH PHILOSOPHER

CHAPTER 6
Bullies

Shery

B ullies deserve a section all their own. Bullies come in all sizes, shapes, and stripes. They are at all levels of an organization, from front line to management to leadership. They are gender agnostic and reside both inside and outside your organization. Oftentimes, bullies make their way up the company ladder because they are technically skilled. And, quite frankly, bullyism has been promoted in management and leadership culture throughout history.

Kelly and I encountered bullies throughout this two-year process of collaborating. There were those whom we considered to be partners, while others appeared as wolves in sheep's clothing—they started out as partners, yet were anything but. Some were better at masking than others, some meaner than others.

When I entered the health care marketing arena, I was hired by a woman who had grown through the hospital ranks into management. What she had in a good heart, she lacked in leadership. Rather than talking with her staff or colleagues, she used sticky notes. My job at the time was to promote the hospital's emergency department. If I needed guidance, a note appeared on my door. If I needed a meeting, I could handle it through adhesive squares. This was in the days before email or Twitter, so perhaps the sticky-note-based hospital vice president was simply training me for coming technology.

Through some departmental reorganization, my position was moved to the marketing department. This was a good fit. The director had a rich history in health care marketing. He was creative and encouraged creativity in his staff. He was eventually recruited by an out-of-town facility, and a new leader was hired. She was a seemingly amiable marketing professional who was well connected in the community, as she was fond of reminding those around her. She savored being the face, heart, body, and soul of all things hospital related. At this point in time, I was running an off-site women's clinic and reporting to the hospital COO, so I figured I'd have few interactions with her.

When a new CEO started at the hospital, the marketing director became so close to this CEO that everyone, including the COO, had to go through *her* to meet with the CEO. My reporting relationship was augmented with a dotted line to marketing. After trying this for a few months, it became apparent that an environment in which I had dual-reporting relationships with minimal access to my primary leader was less than optimal, so I turned in my resignation. The marketing director, being the type of manager who became angry when one of her staff members—even one who was not a direct report—resigned, was unhappy with me.

I arrived at work the day after submitting my resignation to learn she had been through my office the previous evening. I learned of her late-night visit by commencing with my workday, reviewing my to-do list I maintained on a legal pad in a leather padfolio. Starting a new page, I noticed deep writing indentations on this otherwise-clean sheet of paper. The page with the actual writing had been torn out, but the deep etching from the writing remained. The message was strong and clear: a four-letter word followed by "you."

I made an appointment with the COO to convey my concerns and offer to just leave rather than work out my notice period. I arrived early for the meeting with him, so I went to the small office I used when on the hospital campus.

I walked in to find the director behind my desk.

After a terse exchange, I told her I was meeting with the COO and held up my padfolio. I had never experienced a human taking flight before, and this was certainly not the image I had envisioned, but she did it. She came flying over the top of the desk, yelling and grabbing for the pad and me. Shocked, I quickly escaped the office with a minor scratch on my arm but with my pad intact. She was still yelling as I exited the building.

I did not get the opportunity to talk with the COO, nor did I work out my notice. Actually, since the director had the ear of the CEO, only her message came through and resulted in my termination with only one week left to work there. This situation felt difficult and unfair, but there was no unringing that bell.

Fortunately, I soon secured my own marketing-director position with another facility. Memories of how sick a work environment can be fueled my drive to create and promote a workplace where employees are valued for what they do and who they are as people, both inside and outside the office.

I have also experienced the belief by certain people with strong personalities that a leader cannot be caring and empathetic while still being strong. Once, in a hospital meeting of around two hundred managers, the CEO was fielding questions about a contentious subject. The specific topic has lost its significance and slipped from my memory over time, but the scenario imprinted on my mind. After addressing the same question multiple times from the managers, the CEO became frustrated and lost her temper. In an exasperated response, she said she was done with further discussion on the matter. The room went uncomfortably silent, and we soon concluded for the day.

The next morning when we gathered for the final day of the meeting, she apologized to the room for her strong response, stating she could have dealt with her frustration differently. As I sat there admiring the bravery it took for her to do this, her second-in-command leaned over to me and said, "I *told* her not to apologize. It makes her look weak."

In that moment, I wondered how many of the two hundred attendees perceived her apology as weakness and how many, like me, viewed it as true strength.

Not being a psychologist, this is solely my opinion: bullyism looks a lot like sociopathy as most bullies seem to fit somewhere on that end of the spectrum. They want control of all you have and all you are, though you only matter to them depending on what they want from you or what they can get from you. They live by situational rules that are continually changing. These rules are applied when convenient to them or when they will positively serve their desired outcome, yet they expect strict adherence to their rules by others. There is no room for genuine collaboration, no room for ideas or initiatives outside of their own agenda. Some bullies stonewall by ignoring you. Others threaten to retaliate. And all seem to have stories and narratives that are sort of, almost, somewhere near the ballpark of factual and true, stories and narratives that sound reasonably plausible and seem believable to those who are not directly involved. There seems to be a great deal of devotion given to creating alternate realities and spinning those tales with key stakeholders critical to the desired initiatives.

What Kelly and I experienced in our collaborative process from the bullies varied. Throughout our work initiating the strategies of our two physician groups, we met with hospital systems, recognizing that each of these organizations would be impacted by our collaboration. We invited them to be part of what we were doing. Consistently, the responses were around resistance, some passive and some active. One simply avoided calls, texts, and meeting requests of all kinds until we contacted the next level up in the health system. Meanwhile, the other one metaphorically patted us on the heads with an "isn't this cute" response until it came to fruition. As the purchase of the small, independent hospital became real, the cannonballs flew. There were phone calls to our leadership offering to purchase each group. When that failed, the threats escalated. All the long-standing service contracts between the health system and each physician group were summarily terminated. Our physicians, who had been elected to leadership on the medical staff by their physician peers, were sent a letter telling them to resign from their position. Interestingly, the hospital included a draft letter our physician leaders were instructed to send to the medical staff stating how the physician was competing and had a conflict of interest. One physician took exception to this mea culpa draft and wrote his own letter explaining he was being removed from leadership, that resignation was forced on him. He also pointed out that physicians and hospitals have always competed but have always been able to work together for the good of the patient until now because "Goliath was afraid of David."

Kelly and I were told that if the hospital removed payment for those service contracts and removed these physicians from leadership, then we would be pressured into backing down from our strategic direction. Meanwhile, another hospital system, while not happy about physicians owning a small hospital, was more congenial. The leadership team for that system proudly offered their version of collaborative partnerships that would ultimately result in the physician groups becoming hospital employees. Hospital systems across the nation offer partnerships that serve to further their control by weakening or owning the independent physicians, yet there is rarely consideration given to reducing the costs of health care and promoting the health of the community.

Bullies are relentless. They are exhausting. And the ones I have personally encountered attempt to "win" by wearing down those around them. They are dangerous since the good of an organization or initiative is neither their concern nor motivation. They continue to thrive in all environments since there often is not an effective way to move them out of an organization. This is, of course, unless you are their boss or unless they need you for meeting their particular end goals.

In our case, it was through our collaboration that Kelly and I were able to endure and weather the barrage of attacks. When two people experience the same hardship at the same time, a bond is forged. When those same two already hold a similar vision for their organizations, a powerful underpinning is established that is capable of withstanding the pressure of those who would have them fail. Because Kelly and I were fiercely intent in purpose and passion, we remained true on our persistent path toward the best health-care design for our market. We were able to stand strong against the obstinacy of those who would have us fail or become like them.

In dealing with bullies, remember:

- Bullies do not know their own weaknesses. They regard themselves far too highly, leaving their Achilles, heel exposed. Figure out what this Achilles' heel is. Knowledge is power.
- When bullies tried to stop Kelly and me because of the strength of our collaboration, we simply went around another way. There is always a way to do the right thing. When roadblocks arise, regroup and find another way. Where walls are built, remove the bricks. Keep saying "Yes, we can" and yes, you will.
- Bullies will often reveal their plans for your demise since they are prideful and believe themselves to be the smartest in the room. Listen. Bullies tell you what they are going to do next. Sometimes it is in the subtleties of a conversation. Sometimes it is more direct. Listening gives you knowledge you can use to prepare, and whether through precaution, preemption, or response, you will rarely be surprised.
- Sometimes the loudest response is silence. When you engage with bullies, you also risk giving away your methods for dealing with them. Silence is a powerful tool. If they do not know your reaction, they cannot intercept or impede your next steps.
- You likely are not in a position to rid a department or a company of a bully. The best strategy then is to stay out of the line of fire when possible and always hold on to your integrity.
- Do not let the bully deter your plan. Fear can creep in when all the cannons are facing your direction. Stay focused on doing the right thing and good will come.

Be willing to be uncomfortable. Be comfortable being uncomfortable. It may get tough, but it's a small price to pay for living a dream.
—PETER MCWILLIAMS, AMERICAN AUTHOR

CHAPTER 7
More and Less

Shery

This chapter addresses the tricky and sometimes-touchy area of handoff: How do I gracefully become less so the next person can become more? This requires two people with aligned intention and purpose. Two who are willing to give so the end goal remains the organization's best outcome.

President Franklin Delano Roosevelt and his wife, Eleanor, occupied the White House for just over twelve years. During his presidency, he and Eleanor dreamed of an organization where countries could come together rather than wage war against one another. Just months into his fourth term, Roosevelt died and Harry Truman took office.

Recognizing the merits of this dream, President Truman supported the formation of the United Nations. Because Mrs. Roosevelt was a visible and vocal activist for social justice during her tenure as First Lady, President Truman appointed her as the first United States representative to the General Assembly of the United Nations in March of 1946.

One of the first tasks the UN undertook was to create the Universal Declaration of Human Rights. Mrs. Roosevelt's UN colleagues had such great appreciation for her leadership and activism, they appointed her chair of the Human Rights Commission during the drafting of this declaration, which was adopted by the General Assembly on December 10, 1948. Her passion for social justice and universal human rights created the fire in her that produced fuel toward change. The process was incredibly complex. This commission included appointees representing fifty-three countries with one-third of the seats changing each year. It met for the first time in January 1947, and by December 1948, the universal declaration was adopted by the United Nations.[19]

Admittedly, our scenario is not the United Nations, but it did impact lives locally on a large scale. The three strategies—a physician alliance, a merger, and a physician-owned hospital purchase—would provide freedom to the independent physicians who were being squeezed out of the larger, more established hospital systems. Change is difficult, even when it is positive change. For change to be successful, there must be shared vision. The "why" of the change will drive each decision, so it must be clear, well communicated, and repeated often.

As Simon Sinek stated in his book *Start With Why*, we are inspired by the why of what we do, our purpose, the driver of our passion. As challenging as it can be to parse through the how and what we do to discern our why, "gaining clarity of WHY ... is not the hard part. It is the discipline to trust one's gut, to stay true to one's purpose ...."[20]

That is the most difficult part. It is critical to understand that a clear vision alone is not enough. The journey on the way to a realized vision will pivot. It dips and turns, sometimes reversing and other times accelerating. It will not look like the road map originally sketched out in my brain nor the map in Kelly's. Sticking solely to the original plan limits opportunities for creative design necessary to a successful outcome. Determining that there is one way to accomplish a goal produces rigid inflexibility and dampens the creative process. An original plan is shielded from human and environmental factors,

---

19 Patrick Allitt et al., "Eleanor Roosevelt and the United Nations," chap. 13 in *Life, Liberty, and the Pursuit of Happiness: A History of the American Experiment* (Arlington: Bill of Rights Institute, 2020), https://billofrightsinstitute.org/essays/eleanor-roosevelt-and-the-united-nations.

20 Simon Sinek, *Start With Why: How Great Leaders Inspire Everyone to Take Action*, rev. ed. (2009; repr., New York: Penguin Group, 2011), 214.

meaning we can prepare for expected contingencies, but we won't know the actual impact to our plans if and until they happen.

Learning and possessing the ability to pivot prepares us for the unknown. When we come against a wall, do we go around, tunnel under, or break through? There's an unexpected, fast-flowing river ahead. Do we forge across, turn around, or build a bridge? The journey will never go 100 percent according to plan. Embracing the bumps and stumbles as readily as we do the rainbows and vistas promotes an internal, fertile ground for weathering the inevitable challenges.

Along the way, there were many opportunities for Kelly or for me to push the other aside to take credit for an idea or a whole set of ideas. The fact that this did not happen gave our initiatives the greatest opportunity for success. When a leader is focused on taking credit and recognition, which often also involves assigning blame, optimal success of that goal is compromised and may never be reached.

In our situation, our vision was aligned, and our approach to attaining this vision was also aligned. We each took responsibility during those times when the train went sideways, and we were both willing to share in the successes along the way. Make no mistake, it is not easy to hear your words or your ideas conveyed from another's presentation. It is natural and human to take pride in our ideas and actions. When we hear or see someone else using those thoughts or ideas as original to them, there is a pang in the gut. We so often feel the need to prove our value and relevance to our boss, board, peers, or staff. Thinking we gave away the credit we believe we deserve can cause us to feel threatened.

Rather than reacting with that feeling of righteous indignation, redirect your thoughts to your why. By maintaining our focus on our why, our purpose remained our goal, not who got the most credit. In those times where one of us might feel marginalized by the process, we talked about it *with one another*. Please grasp the importance of the relationship of the two key players. We remained in dialogue. This was dialogue *with* one another rather than *about* one another.

All too often, we as humans feel threatened, feel that our idea is being hijacked or stolen, producing a strong likelihood that we will end up undermining the entire process, starting with talk about the other person. One key difference with Kelly and me was our communication. We were purposeful about the information before it was presented to our physicians. In other words, we prepared for meetings and messages by dividing and sharing the flow of the information, using some of Kelly's thoughts and some of mine, with the result of a consistent, unified message and vision. With the powerful strategies we presented, knowing these would disrupt our market since the health systems were so vocal about their opposition, remaining true to our purpose outweighed desire for personal accolades. Stand together. Give a little. Get a lot.

What we did and how we navigated this process required intention. It required our focus to be the true north of the collaboration. In our case, the focus was to do the right thing by creating the best and strongest independent multispecialty clinic that is driven by care for the patient—medically, financially, and emotionally. Each decision could be solidly made on this foundation.

Let's get back to where we started with the United Nations. On the CNN original series *First Ladies*, Christopher Brick, editor and principal investigator on the "Eleanor Roosevelt Papers Project," said of Mrs. Roosevelt, "[She] figured out decades ago that you can get a tremendous amount done if you don't care about taking credit for it."[21]

Whether it is an international organization or two physician groups in America's Midwest, setting personal affirmation and ego aside results in moving mountains.

Successful collaboration is dependent on many factors. Among these are:

- Know and understand your why. Keep it top of mind in each decision, action, and reaction to your initiative. Simon Sinek's *Start With Why* will help you get to the core.

---

21 "The Presidency: First Ladies Symposium," American History TV, C-Span 3, posted May 6 2021, 74 min., https://www.c-span.org/video/?511819-5/ladies-communications.

- When our focus is on the why, it shifts the focus away from distractions that can and will derail the primary goal.
- As difficult as it can be to "give to get," setting aside ego and recognition produces great results.
- Communicate. Communicate your why. Communicate with your collaborator. Refrain from *talking about* and opt for *talking with*. Communication can eliminate the assumption of bad intent on the part of others.
- Be intentional. Be thoughtful.

You never really understand a person until you consider things from his point of view—until you climb into his skin and walk around in it.
—ATTICUS FINCH IN *TO KILL A MOCKINGBIRD* BY HARPER LEE

CHAPTER 8
Culture

Shery

For years, our companies had conversations about merging or working together in some meaningful way. For years, this was rejected because our cultures were so different. One company was created as a decentralized structure to ensure that physicians retained control of their practices. A physician board, elected by each practice, made strategic decisions while operational decisions resided in each of the practices. The other company, on the other hand, was a centralized structure with control residing in the CEO and a few physician leaders. Both cultures have positives and both have negatives.

In a centralized organization, strategic direction and control resides with a few in leadership. Responsibilities, processes, and procedures are standardized across the organization, resulting in more consistency among departments. With centralization, creativity resides with the few at the top. Decisions may be implemented quickly but with more staff resistance when changes have no input from those affected by the change.

In a decentralized model, the few in leadership invite the team to contribute their knowledge, experience, and expertise. Top leadership from the day-to-day operations allow more room for focus on strategic direction. A decentralized organization promotes self-sufficiency and independent thinking, though they often have more variation in processes. However, as organizational changes are introduced, more time is spent gathering input and incorporating that input into the plan. By the time the change is implemented, the team is familiar with it and has had a hand in its development.

When Kelly arrived on the scene in 2018, she immediately began moving her company toward a more decentralized culture. She engaged physician owners and encouraged them to participate in the decisions affecting their organization. She empowered staff with authority and accountability. She began using the physician board of trustees as the primary governing body supported by a committee structure that assisted with problem-solving, driving change, and assessing opportunities.

As we considered bringing these two organizations together, assessing our cultures was of critical importance—truly understanding and appreciating the similarities and the differences. Throughout our careers, Kelly and I had both been through mergers and acquisitions. The knowledge we gained through those experiences along with our independent research said that culture is foremost. It is one of the primary reasons a merger would succeed or fail. As many as 30 percent of mergers fail because of neglect around a meticulous process of bringing two diverse cultures together,[22] so widely communicating and discussing the cultural comparisons between and among our groups was integral and imperative. It is easy to look at larger mergers and acquisitions that have failed and quickly see where a clash of culture played a significant role in an otherwise well-planned strategy.

A prime example of this happened in the years just before Kelly and I embarked on our adventure. Two groups attempted a merger that was a strategic win for both. Both are well known and highly regarded clinically by peers and patients. One has a highly competitive reputation and the other is known for a strong work-and-life balance.

---

22 Frederick D. Miller and Eileen Fernandes, *Cultural Issues in Mergers and Acquisitions* (New York: Deloitte Consulting LLP, 2009), https://www2.deloitte.com/content/dam/Deloitte/us/Documents/mergers-acqisitions/us-ma-consulting-cultural-issues-in-ma-010710.pdf.

These groups have always held to a tacit agreement that neither would enter the other's market, just a county line away. When they began talks of merger, the health-care community watched with interest. The prevailing thought was that it was the perfect strategic idea and a cultural disaster. The two groups, being aware of their differences, spent a couple of years working together, creating and marketing a new name, and combining staff and operations. They even went through the rigors of a Federal Trade Commission investigation to ensure they would not control too much of the market. Within months of pulling the trigger, the merger crumbled. While only the two practices know what happened on the inside, to the market, it appeared that neither organization could or would adopt the culture of the other. Any congeniality that existed prior to the merger vanished, and the two are now actively and openly competing in each other's backyard. Untold investment into the combined company became a sunk cost.

Being aware of the importance of culture, Kelly and I engaged a consultant who specialized in cultural integration to perform an initial culture assessment with the engagement of a joint committee of physicians. This committee, consisting of physician-elected leaders from both organizations, were led through a series of questions designed to distinguish similarities and differences in our two cultures. Questions ranged from governance to operations, autonomy to staff-level decision-making. Through this process, we learned we were much more alike culturally than we had imagined. We then communicated this comparison throughout both organizations, inviting physicians and staff to ask any questions. We held biweekly meetings for this purpose.

In the early meetings, the room was full. Most of the questions centered around "I heard we will lose our 401 (k)"—not true—and similar questions. Within a couple of months, the attendance dwindled to just a few people, and the questions reverted to normal physician-practice operations. We brought together the middle managers multiple times to collaboratively create workflow processes that incorporated knowledge and experience from both organizations.

Leading up to one of these meetings, we began hearing that managers of one company were telling managers of the other that there would be no collaboration around business processes, which created anxiety, mistrust, and even depression. This was going on even though Kelly would meet these types of behaviors head-on.

As the meeting approached, I reached out to Kelly with a plan to see if we could infuse some empathic behaviors. The meeting day arrived, all the attendees got situated, and I kicked off the meeting with an announcement that a decision had been made; we were now going to switch the direction of the merger. Both Kelly and I explained that after looking again at the legal and marketing aspects of the merger, the steering committee and combined boards came to this decision. This, of course, was not the case, but we needed the managers to understand the feeling of merging into another company versus being the company merged into.

This simple exercise had an astounding effect. The observable impact, alone, told Kelly and me there were assumptions being made in both organizations. Some managers responded with wide-eyed surprise followed by a visible lowering of shoulders and loss of eye contact. Other managers had equally wide-eyed surprise, but their shoulders straightened, and their facial expressions were of greater engagement. We continued the rest of the meeting under this premise.

At the end, Kelly and I clarified that, no, this change had not taken place, then we solicited feedback of how managers from each organization felt. There was some reluctance to share at first, though once the discussion started, there was a collective nodding of heads accompanied with people saying, "Oh, I get it now." Kelly and I later shared the experience with the steering committee and combined boards, who also learned from this role-reversal exercise.

Even with all our intentionality around culture, we still encountered hiccups. One situation involved a key employee who was offered a top leadership role in the merged company, though it was not the one she hoped to secure. As the months progressed, it was her role to ensure certain key functions migrated well to the new system. Each time a milestone was expected to be accomplished, she had reasons why it could not be done and would spend hours of time justifying her reasoning. Assuming she was disappointed in her merged role, her new leader provided latitude to allow for adjustment. Instead of engaging with the new team, she began a campaign to sabotage the merger. There were a few physicians who were on the fence about the merger, and these were the ones she contacted. She planted seeds of doubt, which then Kelly or I had to spend critical time unwinding. Concurrently, rather than completing the relevant work needed for the migration, she devoted days to telling managers they would be replaced or their positions consolidated and given to other managers, necessitating additional redirection of my time to disentangle this twisted information.

Once negative seeds are sown, wary fruit is produced. The managers who were fed jaundiced information watched Kelly's actions and mine with caution, measuring that our words and actions matched. Not only was this employee attempting to derail the merger, her coworkers and staff were burdened with picking up her workload while being distracted with her negativity.

As her pattern of delayed productivity and undermining actions appeared as more than discontent with not getting the role she desired, it became evident she needed to move on from our company, "getting her off the bus" as Jim Collins calls it in his book *Good to Great*. In this book, Collins conveyed his team's research findings that having the right people on the bus was found in the great companies. He states:

> The good-to-great leaders understood three simple truths. First, if you begin with "who" rather than "what," you can more easily adapt to a changing world. [...] Second, if you have the right people on the bus, the problem of how to motivate and manage people largely goes away. [...] Third, if you have the wrong people, it doesn't matter whether you discover the right direction; you *still* won't have a great company. Great vision without great people is irrelevant.[23]

---

23 Jim Collins, "Who First ... Then What," chap. 2 in *Good to Great: Why Some Companies Make the Leap ... and Others Don't* (New York: Harper Business, 2001), 42.

Collins's third principle reinforced the need to remove her from our bus. This is never a comfortable decision, even when supporting facts substantiate it. You are affecting someone's life and livelihood, so thoughtfulness is required. However, resist the temptation to procrastinate because of discomfort. Leave the wrong person in place, and opportunities for misbehavior arise, as we clearly saw. At the same time, you run the risk of losing strong employees who are carrying her load and wondering why leadership will not make the change.

Culture work continues long beyond the actual merger. It takes years for merged companies to assimilate the two into one. Some staff and leadership are able to embrace the changes and some will decide to fulfill their career goals elsewhere. This is normal. Yet the culture that emerges is one that reflects the leadership, vision, and heart of the combined organization. Successful mergers prioritize culture. Key considerations for culture integration are:

- To the people who are not in the room where detailed discussions occur, combining cultures is like bringing a new dog into a home with a cat. There is a slow and methodical process for introducing the parties and allowing them time to familiarize themselves with one another. Without taking that deliberate and necessary time, there will be a great deal of hissing and growling.
- The easy parts of a merger are what can be put on a spreadsheet, charted, and graphed. The difficult parts require soft skills which are harder to see and cannot be rushed. Emotion and fear will happen regardless, and it is the leader's job to pay attention and manage these responses.
- Engage a consultant who is trained in organizational change management.
- Seek ways to help each organization understand how the other feels. Take caution against minimizing the feelings of grief, feelings of a fading identity, and feelings of loss of control.

I have not failed. I've just found 10,000 ways that won't work.
—Thomas Edison

CHAPTER 9
Collaboration Gone Sideways

Kelly

I've had a few collaborative efforts in the last year not work out exactly as I thought they would or could have. Such results are to be expected. The key is learning from the experience and, most importantly, knowing when to call it quits.

When working on multiple strategic projects, I often say to my team that we may have several plates spinning—think, *Circus!*—at the same time, but a few are likely going to fall because that is usually the case. Due to my delusional optimism, which we've already thoroughly explored, I'm always a little bummed when a plate crashes, and for a few minutes, I feel a twinge of failure that, ultimately, I do get over quickly. The question is: How do you manage the aftermath of the crash? A great case study is a project that has consumed the last fifteen months of my life and was one of the top-three most important strategic initiatives for the organization I most recently worked for.

It is very common for organizations like ours to have capital partnerships to fund growth. We had reached a size that, in order to scale and grow, we would need a partner. My board agreed, and I set out to do the assessment and find a partner.

These types of partnerships can come in all kinds of different shapes and forms. You start with a clear vision of the type of partner you want—alignment, vision, etc.—define the guardrails or scope—do they acquire you, is it a joint venture, will there be an asset purchase, etc.—and start entertaining companies that may fit with what you are looking for. As I started the assessment, I created a table with multiple channels or types of organizations that could meet our scope and could be aligned with our mission. My CFO and I began meeting with different groups. We signed nondisclosure agreements with each of them and exchanged some data to learn what each of us brought to the table. The different channels included private equity, health systems, payers, and similar medical groups.

As the conversations played out, I began to check off different elements on a pros-and-cons list. The partner who would meet what the physicians were looking for and what the company needed started to become very clear. The challenge was that we had one suitor who became singularly focused on one outcome: acquiring River Valley Medical Group, despite our being crystal clear that we would not be acquired and that our physicians would not be employed. I believed we could still work together even when we declined their offer to purchase the organization. I was incorrect.

Once we declined their offer to purchase our company, and once we chose another partner, this health system launched an aggressive recruitment plan to hire our physicians. Letters were sent to our physicians' homes with promises to personally reach out to them to provide an offer. Several of the physicians received email offers to join their organization. Our board president and I met with the health-system leaders to discuss how we could collaborate, and why, more than ever, we should work together, but we were met with hostility and the promise to continue recruiting our physicians. They were clearly threatened by the capital partner we had chosen and saw this new partnership as a competitive move versus simply what it was.

Where and when did this project get off track, and how could I have done things differently to avoid such a response? It is possible that this was the inevitable outcome; the message we heard from this experience was, "You either join us, or we will crush you." Health systems have deep pockets and can make it difficult for smaller physician groups to sustain aggressive recruitment campaigns like this. Some groups would give in. We will not. Another option might have been to bring both potential partners to the same table and see if there is room for all of us to work together. I may try that in the future.

Another example is one that is still evolving as I write this and is related to our investment in Concordance Hospital. This one hurts a little given the strategic opportunity that I believe still exists for a particular organization. This venture was a collaboration with two other entities in the community, one that is another independent medical group and the other that is an investor in health-care organizations. We spent close to a year discussing the opportunity, the value to the community, and the impact we could have on patient experience. We worked hard to create governance and operating agreements that would ensure fairness and hopefully help us avoid control issues as we moved forward. Committees were set up with equal representation from physicians in both organizations and there was equal representation on the board.

Despite putting into place what we thought were safeguards, a power struggle ensued. It became clear through the discussions around these power struggles that we did not share a common vision for the opportunity. We also did not share the same values, and this truth came out in how we approached issues as well as between interactions with hospital team members and vendors.

As we worked to navigate these issues for close to two years, I began to ask the physicians and leaders if we were accomplishing what we had hoped to with this strategic initiative. The group was torn. While there was acknowledgment that there were issues, folks also felt optimistic that we could overcome them because the opportunity was so great. We were having similar discussions at the board level as well. Ultimately the question became whether these were the right partners for us even if the opportunity itself was still very valid, and ultimately the answer was no, we are not the right partners. There were so many valuable lessons throughout this project, but most importantly, I think it was this one: no partnership can be successful if you do not share the same vision and if your values are not aligned.

The real lesson here is accepting that when you cast a wide net and work to be a community collaborator, sometimes, despite your best efforts, not everyone will want to collaborate with you. Here are ways to support your collaborative efforts:

- Always be clear with your intentions with any organization you are trying to build a relationship with. Be open and transparent about what you are looking for and what you are not interested in.
- Keep communications professional and respectful. Always.
- Meet with your competitors, even when you cannot see any opportunities where your organizations could come together.
- Don't take any of it personally. These types of negotiations can be difficult, but you don't know when you will have the opportunity to try again and work together down the road!
- Try. It might not work out, but you don't know where there are collaboration and partnership opportunities until you reach out and have the conversation.
- Do your own mini-RCA—root-cause analysis—when a project doesn't end the way you hoped. Assess opportunities to do things differently next time.
- Pivoting away from one opportunity to another is not failure, it is making a smart and well-thought-out business decision to focus your time and resources in the direction that will bring the most value.

Don't set yourself on fire to keep someone else warm.
—A<small>NONYMOUS</small>

CHAPTER 10
Gaslighting and Other Toxic Behaviors

Kelly

There's an old country music song by Kenny Rogers that is running through my head as I start to write this chapter. In "The Gambler," he sings about how it's critical to know when to hold a hand of cards and when to "fold 'em." Don't worry, this will make more sense as you read on.

I was introduced to Sally, a local business woman, shortly after coming to the community. Sally had begun to work with physician-owned practices. She was well connected and sat on several community business boards. When we began discussing a joint venture opportunity with another independent physician group in town, the group brought Sally to the table as a possible investor.

During these investment meetings, Sally certainly spoke with authority and confidence and clearly had the trust of some of the physicians. Add all of this up, and it was not hard to see why she had been successful. While her ego challenged me, she knew the business and had the trust of the physician group we were partnering with, so we moved ahead with this joint venture opportunity. Shortly after this investment deal closed, I began to see exactly how Sally operated and often manipulated situations to gain control.

In this new venture, my role was to ensure the business operations were launched and care was provided safely and efficiently. There was a lot of work to do to turn the business around, but we had a plan and began to see improvements. Sally was a board member and also a member of the finance committee, which was an ideal place for Sally to participate given her business background. Unfortunately, she rarely attended meetings where we would review financials in preparation for board meetings. Instead, she would use her position on the board to question the validity of financial statements. I'd ask her to join the committee meetings so we could address her questions and concerns, and she would agree to attend and then never followed through. Every month at the board meeting, she would question the numbers, planting doubt into other board members' minds as well.

This pattern of behavior was confusing to me until her intentions finally became clear when she asked that the organization consider implementing a business solution she owned into this new joint venture. Sally had been making her case for the need by degrading the financial performance of the organization, yet she would not participate in regular financial discussions. Instead of making an honest pitch for the business, she was absent from those important finance meetings and then followed up by pointedly questioning the financial integrity of the business. These arrows she shot at the informational integrity, while initially cloaked in concern, soon appeared fully clothed in the effort to win a contract. Despite my best efforts, including petitioning the board to complete a request-for-proposals process, I could not stop it. The board voted to implement her service, and my team felt degraded and unsupported as a result. I wish I could have prevented this, but even though Sally had been invalidating data or information to get something she wanted or to make a point she'd had for some time, I hadn't initially seen her scheme. Looking back, I realize now Sally used this same approach multiple times to get her way. She was also a gaslighter.[24] The story I shared earlier

---

24 *Gaslighting* is a form of emotional manipulation used to control another person. For example, a gaslighter will work to get their victims to doubt themselves, their work, their memory, etc. I had never heard this term until I was talking to Shery about Sally's behavior, and she said, "Well, she is

about Sally invalidating the financials is a good example. I have thirty years of experience in revenue-cycle work, but after many difficult conversations where this data was continually being questioned, I began to question myself. I often asked myself, *What could I be missing?* Sally used this behavior to gain control as well. By getting other leaders to question their own expertise, she could step in and take control. Gaslighting is abusive behavior.

Earlier in my career, a good friend helped me to see how unhealthy it is to work in a situation or for an organization I did not share the same value system with. As a younger leader, being in these types of situations would make me question myself. Essentially, I would wonder what it was about *me* that caused the relationship to fail, or why *I* couldn't work with this person or in this situation.

Another similar situation was with a peer on an executive team at a large health system. This coworker was a finance leader and seemed very challenged by the growth plans I brought forward. I worked hard to share detailed versions of plans and ask for his input to help gain alignment, but continued to hear from our CEO that this leader had ongoing concerns and conveyed negative critique about my work. This leader had the ear of the CFO and board members and would openly criticize my projects or presentations in board meetings. I spent a lot of time and energy trying to get on the same page and find alignment but could never get there. I blamed myself for not being able to reach a healthy place with this leader. He was eventually let go as these issues were not just with me and were having a negative impact on the organization.

As I've matured in my career, I've begun to see unhealthy work situations or business relationships differently. I can now recognize when my values don't match the values of the organizations or that of an individual business partner I work with. Most importantly, I'm no longer willing to compromise my own values. Sometimes, the only way to fix the situation is to move on, unless you are willing

---

a gaslighter."

to change your own value system. Sally and I do not share the same values, and I am *not* going to compromise my values to make a business venture work. I've put a lot of energy into trying to understand others' intentions and improve the situation. Sometimes, knowing when to "fold 'em" is the most important thing to know.

I will not continue to subject myself or my team to these types of behavior and will walk away when needed. Did I fail in this venture? I don't feel like I did. Rather, I feel empowered to stand up for what I know is right, and more importantly, I feel I am at a place where I can really set boundaries to protect myself, my team, and the organization. In the past, I likely would have felt like I "had" to make this work and continue to subject myself to the unhealthy behavior. I also would have blamed myself instead of recognizing behavior that's toxic and choosing to walk away from it. But now, I am choosing to *not* be a victim and to protect myself and the organization from someone who does not have our best interest in mind. This is the best position of all.

Key takeaways:

- Trust your instincts and intuition about people. If something doesn't feel right, move on.
- Don't compromise your values for anyone or any reason.
- These types of behaviors rarely get better, and they are not your fault or your doing.
- Walk away from unhealthy situations or people. To do so is not a failure but a choice to not accept unethical or bad behavior. Walking away can be empowering!

We must be willing to let go of the life we planned so as to have the life that is waiting for us.

—JOSEPH CAMPBELL

CHAPTER 11
The Aftermath

Shery

I love being retired. It is everything I planned, hoped, and dreamed it would be. I am a bit too busy, but I will figure that out eventually. I started my career in health care by introducing emergency-room services, promoting women's health services, and marketing residential rehab for traumatic-brain-injury survivors. I returned to graduate school to gain knowledge of health care operations and leadership to propel a career choice that could weather business and industry cycles. It was there where my passion for physician independence trickled from a brook into a stream.

Over the subsequent thirty years, with tributaries of life, leadership, and industry knowledge converging, the stream became a river. This rushing waterway carried me through times of change and challenge. My desire to obtain a better way to provide services, lead colleagues, and relate to competitors was my energy, my joy.

In 2014, there was a shift: a grandchild. At the same time, this part of my family moved seven hundred miles away, and a new introspection began. With the experience of having lived life's fragility firsthand, I committed to embrace a world beyond health care.

By 2016, I began to recognize the ten-to-twelve- to sometimes eighteen-hour workdays and being "on" seven days a week for a decade was amazing for a season of my life, though now it was time to recede and allow navigation of the rushing waters to be handed over to another. I decided I would retire in my early sixties while I am still healthy and energized by life. This gave me about four years to find or create a way to hand off the organization I loved to someone who had a similar passion.

And so began my succession and postretirement planning.

In 2018, Kelly was recruited to run the area's largest independent-physician group. I reached out to her to introduce myself and the community. This had been done for me by a competitor earlier in my career. It was such an impactful gesture, I added it to my professional toolbox. Kelly graciously accepted, and by the time we concluded our first breakfast meeting, we had plans for pursuing collaborative work, even though we were competitors. It was also at that meeting where I heard the first trickle running toward fulfillment of a sound succession plan. In Kelly, I found another who was fiercely committed to physician independence, experienced in navigating the physician groups among and between rapidly flowing, narrow switchbacks of the health systems. I had found my replacement, and the rivers converged.

Near the end of 2020, our companies were merged, and I was retired right on schedule.

From long hearing the stories of how so many people retire and feel lost or retire and move to a place where their social structure needs to be rebuilt, I chose to stay in my hometown where I have friends and engagement in the community. This has proven to be a rich decision for me. I am immersed in church, in family and friends, and in travel.

Over these last two years, I hiked Glacier National Park, toured Mammoth Cave with grandchildren, kayaked Picture Rocks in Michigan's Upper Peninsula, wandered through the beauty of Denmark and Sweden, and met new family in Ireland. A spirit-renewing mission trip in Guatemala and glorious family week at Disney rounded out my transition into retirement. To feed my residual professional appetite, I serve on the boards of a health plan, a community clinic, and a respite hospital for medically fragile children. Meanwhile, I am working with other professionals in building leadership forums. Remaining in the community where I have spent the last twenty years, I have built friendships with work colleagues, some of whom remained in the organization I left. Good, solid friendships. However, the nature of the friendships must change upon departure. I am no longer available to address problems or fix issues current employees feel. Any expectation otherwise leaves one or both of us frustrated and unfulfilled.

The organization from which I retired no longer exists, and since the planned merger, Kelly has been very busy growing even newer partnerships. The environment and structure has and continues to change for people in both organizations since I left. This is expected since it is under new leadership. As like minded as Kelly and I are, we are of course not the same person, meaning the organization under her guiding hand will be run in her image. Even the doctors I worked with have experienced transformation as they now think through the lens of a corporation versus through their individual practices. And now the question I hear often is whether Kelly and I were being fully transparent about what the company would look like after the merger. With the knowledge and the information we had at the time, our communications were transparent and open. For employees who are grappling with changes, this question is borne out of grief, loss, and unmet expectations. Some changes may be perceived, some may be real.

When these employees first started their jobs, did they perform exactly as the people before them, or did they make their jobs their own? Perhaps the questions should actually be: Am I willing to embrace "new"? Am I willing to grow with the company that has tripled in size with our merger and grown now to a multistate physician group that is large, powerful, and independent?

Just as the river's shoreline changes with each season, so the company I left changes in each new corporate season. The initiatives Kelly and I put in motion shore up and strengthen the long-term survival of this independent group. The reality is that change usually comes upon us rapidly and significantly.

When Kelly and I were operationalizing the strategic plans of our groups, collectively, our physicians were like Frodo Baggins protecting the gold ring of independence while fending off the barrage of attacks coming out of Mordor. The attackers attempted multiple tacks, from ingratiating friendships as a means of carrying out their strategy to systematically assimilate independent-physician groups—watch for those who are not what they seem—to outright threatening miserable defeat for our own strategies and companies if we pursued our plans that would compete with them. The physicians Kelly and I worked with saw the clearest, best path forward was to do this together. Whether we merged our companies, we purchased a hospital, or our physicians became employees of a hospital system, there would be change.

Perhaps the underlying question is whether the lack of employees' expectations being met in transition is less about truth and lies than it is about adaptation. No one manages the same. Market forces change. New personalities become integrated. Much like within a family when you introduce a new pet, get married, or have a child, the family dynamics change as some new component is added. Within our families, we accept these things because we are in control, and they are our choices. When what happens in my workplace is beyond my control, it feels wrong. It can even feel like I am being lied to. We tend to hold on to these perceived wrongs, and the pressure-valve release of talking about them makes us feel better. But we need to exercise caution around the extent to which we enlist others to our side. Certainly, seeking support gives us a sense of control; "We are the resistance for the good of keeping things as they have always been" becomes the rallying cry. And yet, once you see others thriving around you, you might wonder why you were overlooked for a particular project or promotion. You may again feel slighted, the narrative becomes cyclical, and you likely will feel more and more discontentment until something drastic happens.

The great news is we have some ability to affect our story, even when we don't feel in control of it. Change is hard. Change is inevitable. Good will come from change. Recognize you may not get to be in every meeting; certain decisions may now fall on the shoulders of someone else. You have the choice to embrace what is coming your way. Take it on. Reframe your narrative. Recognize what direction the company is going. You have four choices: First, you can dig in your heels through passive resistance. Second, you can rally the troops through active resistance. Third, you can embrace the change and figure out how you can become part of the future. Two of these are the paths of least resistance. Negativity and finding fault are always easier. Initially, anyway. Only one of these options will place you on new ground. It will elevate your spirit and begin to free some of the anxiety that holds your head and heart captive. You may even find that you thrive in this new environment far beyond what you could have imagined. And finally, the fourth option is to depart. There are times when cognitive dissonance is so strong, the best decision is to make a clean break and forge your path elsewhere. Though this, too, is change, it is change that is controlled by you, likely making it more comfortable to adopt.

As you determine your aftermath, resist the negative. Be intentional about your attempt to grasp what is new. Experiencing change is experiencing loss. Whether the change is good or bad, there is a loss of what was. It is normal to feel anger and sadness when we liked what we had and now it is different. It is healthy to work through it. Find a safe way and place to express your grief and sense of loss. And then, find a positive way to deal with it. Lean into the change. When you stay in the grief, you get locked into the negativity that surrounds it. There are always those people who thrive on negativity. They are easy to find, and I believe they naturally gravitate toward one another. Being negative and being around negativity is nonproductive as well as detrimental to your mental health and professional goals. Seek out a positive outlet. Grasp on to embracing the change and explore how you can be a factor in making it better.

No! It is not easy.

No! It is not what you want.

But form follows function so strongly that as you willfully change your attitude, you one day realize your heart is lighter. You are engaged and recognized as you are lifting yourself and others up. As inevitable change occurs in our lives and careers, how we choose to adapt and engage with change impacts our emotional and mental health. It is critical to understand that:

- Change is a loss. Expect anger, frustration, and grief as natural responses.
- What may be perceived injustices may merely be unmet expectations.
- There *is* personal responsibility in feeling happiness and satisfaction. Some changes may warrant recalibration in my point of view, while other changes may warrant leaving for an opportunity better suited to me. I always have a choice.
- What we do with feelings about change defines our own personal paths and legacies. Choose the high road and avoid the hallway confabs of disgruntlement, opting for productive discourse.

Leadership and learning are indispensable to each other.
—JOHN F. KENNEDY

CONCLUSION

Kelly

Obstacles and barriers will invariably get in our way over the course of our careers. These can either overpower us or become the stepping stones to a stronger, better path. As my mom used to tell me, "You cannot control what other people do or how they will act, you can only control your response." Sage advice.

In this book, we've outlined some of these barriers that can get in the way of meaningful change, collaboration, and innovative disruption. We could not control those factors, so we chose to respond to them with persistence in the face of doubt, fear, bullies, unhealthy cultures, and a healthcare system that does not incentivize change.

As mentioned in an earlier chapter, I once reported to a CEO who called me the "great collaborator," and I'm pretty sure he did not mean that in a positive way. For some, collaboration is seen as a weakness. At the time, I was worried my collaborative approach would hold me back as I continued to pursue what I thought was a seat at the right table to drive positive change. As I gained experience, however, I came to realize this is the exact right quality that would help me succeed.

These last two years in particular have shown me what is possible when one is simply willing to say yes and explore these possibilities versus focusing on all the reasons why "it" is impossible or just won't work. Be willing to collaborate and explore relationships that on the surface may seem at odds. The physician groups Shery and I supported were competitors, and for some of our physicians, the thought of us coming together seemed impossible. Today, these same organizations are now fully merged—perhaps not perfect, but together and improved.

We started down this path by having the conversations with our physicians that usually began with the simple question, What if we came together? These early tough conversations helped us talk through the old and complex histories between our organizations, and then we could focus on what could be. The market helped us as well. With the health systems' aggressive behavior against community-based physicians, our two groups also realized we were stronger together than we were apart. This created a joint vision for the future that, ultimately, led to our merger.

I was recently asked with whom I choose to collaborate? In the moment, my answer was "Everyone." My approach has always been to cast a wide net and see what develops. Sometimes, I have an idea of where there might be opportunities to work with another organization, but more often than not, it is through discussion and relationship building that with whom to form a partnership becomes clear.

Shery and I brought two organizations together that had long histories of fierce competition because we knew, despite the past, the future would be better if we came together. It has not been an easy path, but it was the right path. Our hope is that, for years to come, independent physician practices will become stronger together for the good of the community. Sometimes, when meeting with this now-merged group of physicians, I would catch myself thinking about how much we accomplished. It truly has been one of the great joys of my career to see this effort come to fruition and to meet and work with Shery Roussarie. We met shortly after my start with the River Valley Care Providers, and despite our companies being competitors, Shery immediately supported me during my transition into this new community, and we began collaborating and looking for opportunities to drive positive change. I left my very first discussion with Shery with a long list of opportunities we planned to work on together. We did not allow our egos to get in the way of moving forward with initiatives that would bring important changes that we knew would benefit our physicians, our teams, and the community. I learned grace and poise from her, including from the way she cared for the physicians and staff she supported. I found the mentor in Shery I did not have earlier in my career, and I am forever grateful for the opportunity to work with and learn from her. I've since left my work in this community but the learnings have been tremendous and I will carry them with me forever.

Shery

Admittedly, collaborations such as the one Kelly and I formed are infrequent. Business history is full of the one-upmanship of competition—Edison and Westinghouse; American Online (AOL) and Yahoo; not to mention the current space race among Musk, Bezos, and Branson. Kelly and I recognize the rarity of what we accomplished. We also recognize that it does not have to be so.

Competition is good. It makes us strong and better as we continually step up our game to be the best. When the time arrives in the life cycle of an industry, community, or business where the most good can be derived by working together, engage in exploring the world of opportunities that a collaborative option opens. Kelly and I found this in our industry and community. We also found it in each other. Readily we identified our aligned thinking and our aligned goals, and we maximized these shared values. When we were still representing separate companies, we continued to compete while we continued to build a dialogue toward a shared vision. In our vision, we were not some "Pollyanna," believing all would be easy. We predicted and planned for the obstacles that we could and we pivoted and recalibrated in the unexpected. We learned from one another (I believe myself to be the greatest recipient by learning from Kelly's knowledge, experience, and spirit) and we created something big, something amazing.

Our hope for you is that from these stories and experiences, you can see that if you stay focused on doing the right thing, remain persistent despite the challenges that will come your way, and remain open to what is possible, the opportunities are endless!

SHERY'S ACKNOWLEDGMENTS

This adventure of turning the stories in my head from a stream of consciousness into a coherent, meaningful tale could only have been done by the skillful hands and knowledge of Warren Publishing. Mindy, Melissa, Amy, Karli, and Monika, your patience and guidance has been invaluable.

To Collin, my son, the air on which I can soar, and to Sarah, his wife and my best partner in crime, you two are the team who knows me best and have guided me with your insight and wisdom.

To my best friend Debbie who sees me through encouraging and uplifting eyes through which I can never see myself.

To my sisters, Cyndi and Stacee, who have been by my side, simultaneously laughing and praying this life through.

To my husband, Colm, whose heart and love inspire me daily.

I am grateful to those in my life who have taught me and led me by your example––Carol, Carl, Dan, Dave, Jenna, Sarah, Tim, and so many more. Your friendship and leadership makes a difference.

And to Kelly, thinking back on the energy generated as we imagined the future, only with you could all the years of "no" have turned into "yes!" You are the embodiment of possibilities becoming reality. May our lessons learned inspire and encourage others to collaborate creatively, seek surprising solutions, and work for the betterment of the whole.

–Shery

KELLY'S ACKNOWLEDGMENTS

Writing has always been a passion, and I am so incredibly grateful to everyone in my life who has made this dream come true.

To my children——Nicole, Brendan, Natalie, and Brittany——I am so blessed to be your mom and grateful for the daily inspiration you have provided me to do better and fight for what is right. Your own journeys continue to be inspirational, as I have had the blessing to watch you become the amazing human beings you are.

Daren, my husband, thank you for loving and supporting me on this crazy and winding thirty-two-year journey. You believed in me when I didn't believe in myself. I will be forever grateful for you.

I've had the blessing to meet and worked with so many amazing leaders over the course of thirty years. The learnings will stay with me. I am thankful for every single lesson.

To the physicians and providers I've had the absolute pleasure of being able to support, I will always be in awe of the work you do every day. I saw true selflessness during the pandemic and watched you put patients and the community above yourselves. From an early age, I saw my own father, Dr. Michael Macken, give so much of himself for his patients, and that has always inspired me. Thank you for your sacrifice, and I will continue to do my best to support this work and mission.

To Shery Roussarie, thank you for modeling what true grace, empathy, and professionalism looks like in a leader. We crossed paths at the exact time I needed to learn more of these lessons.

My hope is that sharing our journey and lessons learned will help others as they face similar challenges.

Gratefully,
Kelly

CPSIA information can be obtained
at www.ICGtesting.com
Printed in the USA
JSHW020925290323
39629JS00002B/176